TROUT
F I S H I N G
IN NORTH GEORGIA

A Comprehensive Guide
to Public Streams and Rivers

Jimmy Jacobs

PEACHTREE PUBLISHERS, LTD.
Atlanta

Acknowledgments

My sincere gratitude is extended to all those who spent time wandering aimlessly through the North Georgia mountains with me, never knowing we were actually doing research. Thanks also to those who provided inspiration, encouragement and support.

BILL BALDY

JIM COLWELL

REINHARD MOLGEDEI

DON PFITZER

LEROY POWELL

RUSSELL STEPHENS

THEO TITUS

BOB TOWNSEND

JOHN TRUSSELL

BILL VANDERFORD

Published by
PEACHTREE PUBLISHERS, LTD.
494 Armour Circle, NE
Atlanta, Georgia 30324

BOOK DESIGN: CANDACE J. MAGEE
MAPS: DOUGLAS J. PONTE
INTERIOR ILLUSTRATIONS: ROBERT HARRIS

Manufactured in the United States of America

10 9 8 7 6 5 4 3 2

Library of Congress Cataloging-in-Publication Data

Jacobs, Jimmy.
    Trout fishing in North Georgia: A Comprehensive Guide to Public Streams and Rivers / Jimmy Jacobs.
        p.   cm.
    ISBN 1-56145-076-6
    1. Trout fishing—Georgia.   I. Title.
SH688.U6J33   1992   92-43584
799.1'755—dc20   CIP

TO MA and JAKE
for starting me off as a fisherman,

and
TO CATHI
who never let me believe it was impossible

Changes Since the First Printing

In our modern world, about the only thing that does not change is the fact that we are constantly subjected to changes. *Trout Fishing in North Georgia* is not excluded from this trend. As a result of the actions of state fisheries managers, highway engineers, and the U.S. Postal Service, a few updates are needed to the following text. Some of these are rather insignificant from the standpoint of the angler, while others are more substantive.

In the realm of minor changes, since March of 1993 the Georgia Game and Fish Division that manages the trout streams has changed its name to the Wildlife Resources Division (WRD). That same agency also has discontinued publishing the *Guide to Georgia Trout Regulations* pamphlet, adding the information it contained to the *Georgia Trout and Freshwater Sport Fishing Regulations*.

In the discussion of the Chattahoochee WMA, a couple of references are made to the old trout checking stations located there. These stations are no longer in the WRD's inventory of property and have been deleted from maps of the area. Also, regarding directions to the streams on this WMA, GA 356 is mentioned as the road running west from GA 75 at Robertstown. This road is now designated "GA 75 Alternate."

The Postal Service contributed to the changes in this book by moving the Crandall Post Office, mentioned as a landmark in finding the Conasauga River, to a new location on US 411. Fortunately, the intersection where the old post office was located now has a sign providing directions to Lake Conasauga via FS 630.

In addition to these rather minor alterations, a couple of major changes have taken place on the trout streams of the state. Most important is the purchase of a new stream. Wildcat Creek on the Dawson Forest WMA is a feeder stream to the Amicalola River and is accessible via Amicalola Church Road. A long stretch of the headwaters of this wild trout stream runs through 2,000 acres of land purchased in late 1993 and added to the WMA.

Another major change has been the stocking of rainbow trout fingerlings in the Chattahoochee River below Morgan Falls Dam. This stocking is the first of that species in at least fifteen years. As a result, the lower portion of the tailwater on the Hooch reclaims its former status as the best flyfishing water in Georgia.

Jimmy Jacobs
March 1994

Contents

List of Maps

Introduction

Although I grew up in Atlanta, deep in the heart of Dixie where the largemouth bass is king, I spent my youth reading the likes of Corey Ford and Ted Trueblood. I voraciously devoured outdoor magazine tales of rising trout, hatches matched, and hook-jawed, brutish brown trout. While my classmates neglected their studies to dream of hawg-sized bass inhaling plastic worms, my own daydreams revolved around visions of delicate trout rising to a perfectly cast grey hackle peacock in a stream barely wider than a footpath.

In spite of this natural inclination to cold water fisheries, I one day discovered myself to be a college student without ever having actually caught or even fished for a trout. Even sadder, all my dreams had revolved around names like the Beaverkill, Yellowstone, and Au Sable. I was in my early twenties before I discovered that members of the Salmonidae family made their home barely sixty miles north of me in my home state.

Once discovered, however, I dedicated myself to their pursuit with a passion. Although I had been fishing for bluegill with a fly rod since my early teens, as practice for the day I would challenge the trout for which that gear was intended, I opted to use ultralight spinning gear on my first trout ventures in Georgia.

On a bright April day in 1971 I traveled to Cooper Creek north of Dahlonega for the opening day of trout season and the beginning of what has become a lifelong quest for me. My first day on the water I joined the elbow-to-elbow crowd on that heavily stocked and fished creek. The roads were like crowded parking lots, the anglers were out in force, and the fish were reluctant to strike my small spinners. By the end of the day I had managed to land one 7 1/4-inch brown trout. I had also fallen victim to an affliction from which I hope never to recover: I am a trout-fishing addict. For that I make no apologies.

Probably the most frustrating part of my own introduction to trout fishing in Georgia's mountain streams was the sheer lack of solid information about those waters. The Department of Natural Resources' Game and Fish Division published a brochure, complete with map, showing the creeks and rivers that contain trout. They continue to publish that brochure today, and over the years it has been a help to me and many others. There is, however, much that the folder does not tell you.

The map will get you close to most of the streams, but do not always count on it to get you all the way there. Some roads are not on the map, and some that are on the map are marked quite differently when you encounter them in the wild. Also, the map does not give you a hint as to which waters are public and which are on private land. In trout angling this distinction can mean the difference between a good day of fishing and an unpleasant encounter with an annoyed landowner.

Finally, all trout water in Georgia is not the same. Streams have very different personalities. Some are perfect for flycasting, while others will drive you to distraction if you tackle them with a long rod. The latter, with their canopy of overhanging foliage, just beg for an ultralight spinning rig.

All too often, I have met folks in Georgia who profess to be trout anglers. Upon closer questioning, they finally admit to being Cooper Creek anglers or Tallulah River anglers or connoisseurs of some other single stream. Usually their single-mindedness is the result of simple lack of knowledge about the other streams that are available in the state.

Early on I also stuck to a couple of favorite streams, but eventually I began to wander. On many days I spent more time looking for a certain stream I had set out to fish than actually fishing it. Other times I had to consult the maps at the end of the day to figure out that I had been fishing on a creek other than the one for which I had set out.

It is in hopes of saving some other angler problems such as these that I began to put this book together. Even though I have the same natural desire as most fishing enthusiasts to keep my favorite streams to myself, I also know that wild places only exist where there is a constituency that wants them to remain wild. I hope the readers of this work will join me in appreciating these waters and protecting them for the future. That will suit me fine as long as we all do not pick the same stream to fish on the same day next season.

GEORGIA TROUT WATERS

In all, more than 4,100 miles of brooklets, creeks, and rivers are listed as trout waters in the Peach State. Of those, 1,500 miles are primary trout waters in which the fish can survive and reproduce naturally. Most of the rest are marginal waters that are stocked occasionally when the conditions are conducive to supporting trout. Geographically, the streams that contain trout for at least some part of the year are found north of an imaginary line running from Bremen in Haralson County east to Powder Springs in Cobb County, then north to Waleska in Cherokee County. From there the line would turn east again and continue to Lavonia in Franklin County near Lake Hartwell.

Within this range, the primary trout streams can be found in a more confined area along the northern rim of the state. Roughly speaking, these waters are east of US 411 in Murray County. The southern boundary begins at US 76 from Chatsworth in Murray County, east to Ellijay in Gilmer County. From there it would lie north of a cresent-shaped line from Ellijay to Dahlonega in Lumpkin County, to Cleveland in White County, and on to the US 76 bridge over the Chattooga River in Rabun County at the border with South Carolina. As with any arbitrarily drawn boundary, there may be some

Georgia Trout Waters

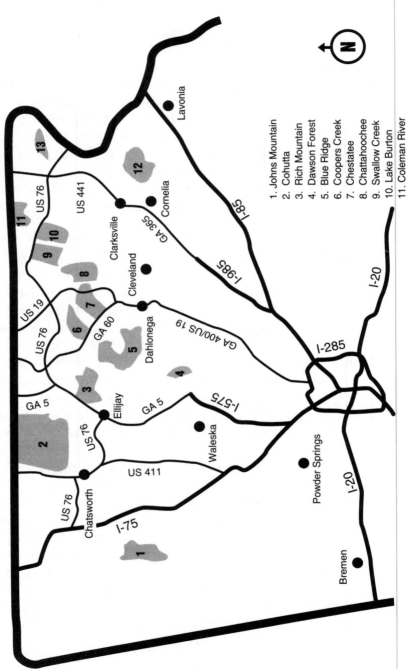

1. Johns Mountain
2. Cohutta
3. Rich Mountain
4. Dawson Forest
5. Blue Ridge
6. Coopers Creek
7. Chestatee
8. Chattahoochee
9. Swallow Creek
10. Lake Burton
11. Coleman River
12. Lake Russell
13. Warwoman

exceptions to these generalizations, but they would be few.

Aside from the classes of streams already mentioned, there is one other variety of moving water that holds trout in Georgia and does not adhere to these imaginary boundaries. The state has three tailrace fisheries - waters below hydroelectric plants - for trout that produce fish year-round, two of which are found south of the lines already detailed. The tailrace water below Buford Dam at Lake Lanier is very well known in the state as an excellent trout stream all the way down to the northern city limits of Atlanta. Lesser-known streams of this type are the waters below Lake Blue Ridge on the Toccoa River in northwest Georgia and the flow below Lake Hartwell on the Savannah River along the border with South Carolina.

These tailrace rivers will contain trout year-round, but they lack the type of water necessary for the fish to spawn. Large numbers of hatchery fish are released in these rivers and many trout will carry over to the next season if not caught.

With this wide variety of trout rivers, streams, creeks, and brooklets in North Georgia, trout anglers are blessed with a large number of options as to where and how to fish for their favored prey. In fact, it would be impossible to cram information about all of the state's trout waters—public and private— into one book. There are just too many places to wet a hook.

RECOMMENDED DESTINATIONS

Because information about waters on private land is useless to the average angler, this book will concentrate on the streams of North Georgia that are on public land or are open to the public for fishing. Many of these are within the boundaries of the Chattahoochee National Forest (NF), which stretches across more than 700,000 acres of mountain land north of Atlanta. Most attention will be focused on the creeks that lie in the Chattahoochee NF and are also contained in one of the state's number of Wildlife Management Areas (WMA). After more than twenty years of trout fishing, I have concluded that the public trout waters of Georgia contain more than a lifetime of angling for those who wish to pursue it.

In looking for an orderly manner in which to discuss the most important trout fishing on Georgia's managed lands, several criteria have been considered. The most obvious is the access available to the public. For that reason, and for ease of organizing the information, the following chapters will be broken down by WMA. In general, public access to these lands is excellent, but there are exceptions. For instance, the book will not include the waters on the Coosawattee WMA in Gilmer and Murray counties. Although there are several streams on the WMA that have trout, the area is broken into so many private parcels of land closed to the public that it is virtually unfishable.

Another criterion that comes into play when looking at any particular management area is the size of the waters. Virtually all of the streams discussed have a number of small feeder creeks that enter them. These brooklets often contain some excellent and untouched trout fishing. Because of their small size, however, they would be crowded if more than one person fished them on any given day. For that reason, we will leave it to the more industrious anglers to find these creeks on their own, and confine discussion to waters that are large enough to handle more than one angler at a time. In some cases where several of these small feeders are located in close proximity to each other they will be mentioned, because, as a group, they offer enough angling water to accommodate several rods.

Ordinarily, the first few seasons of trouting in any new area can be very frustrating as one searches in a hit-or-miss fashion for accessible waters. Especially for the newcomer to the sport of trout angling, but also for the veteran, the following chapters should make trout fishing in Georgia more productive and more fun.

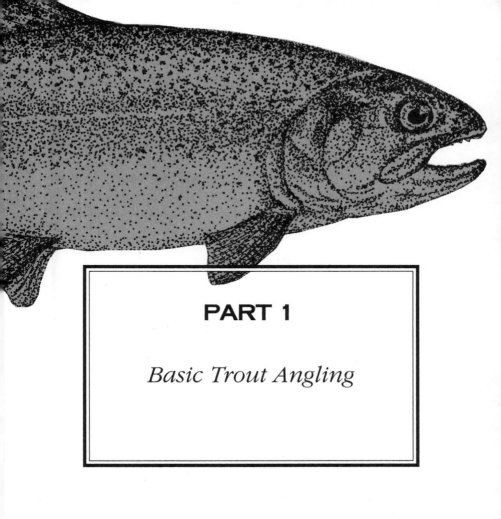

PART 1

Basic Trout Angling

CHAPTER ONE

The Trout

THE BROOK TROUT

When the first European settlers set foot in the Southern Appalachian Mountains the fish they found inhabiting the high-altitude, cold-water streams of the area were native brook trout. In spite of their name, the small, brightly colored fish are not a true trout. They are actually a member of the char family. Regardless of their pedigree, to the early mountaineers they were specs, natives, or simply trout.

Varying in color from dark olive to almost black on their backs, brookies are easily identifiable by the vermicular, or "worm-track," design of the markings on the upper portion of the body. The spots along the side are also helpful in identifying the species. They include a number of red spots surrounded by a halo of color (aureoles) that can range from a light blue to almost lavender.

Over the years there have been occasional flare-ups of the argument over whether the Southern Appalachian branch of the eastern brook trout (*Salvelinus fontinalis*) family should be classified as a separate subspecies. While there are very noticeable differences in coloration and number of spots between the native fish and hatchery-reared brookies that are often stocked in Georgia streams, that question is much too complicated to be dealt with here.

From their original position of dominance in the streams of the southern highlands, brook trout have suffered a fate that closely parallels that of the native people inhabiting these same mountains. Like the Cherokee Indians, the brook trout have been pushed out of their ancestral home by encroaching immigrants. The European brown trout and the rainbow trout from the the west coast of North America, introduced to the area during the twentieth century, have found the region's streams quite hospitable.

These two interlopers have also proven to be much better suited to the creeks of Appalachia, including Georgia, in the sense that they are more adaptable to the changing conditions of this century. Warmer water temperatures and greater silting due to the removal of virgin, first-growth timber are situations that rainbow trout are able to endure better than brookies. At the same time, brown trout are much better than brookies at holding their own against competing warm-water fish in streams at lower elevations.

Brook trout, which will spawn between September and December each year, must have water that remains below 70° F. year-round in order to thrive. In fact, temperatures of 77° F. and higher are lethal to these fish. The ideal range of water temperatures for brookies is from 57° to 60° F. These conditions are found today only in headwater streams, above 2,000 feet in elevation in Georgia.

Besides their water-temperature requirements brook trout have other disadvantages. They rarely attain much size because they have a relatively short 4- to 7-year life span, and a fish of more than 4 years of age is rare. Of every 10,000 brookie fry hatched, only 25 will reach 4 years old, and of these, a single fish will attain an age of 6 years.

Brookies are more prone to feed on insects than other trout species, and they are not wary feeders. Thus, they are easily caught while still juveniles. This is especially true of hatchery-reared fish, which, research has shown, often take as long as four months in the stream before they begin to seek cover or hug the bottom like wild fish.

One other comment on their feeding habits is probably in order at this point. Although brook trout have a reputation for being basically subsurface feeders, they show no real reluctance to rise to floating insects. Probably the fact that they inhabit small headwaters where substantial insect hatches are nonexistent explains this misconception. They simply do not have the opportunity for surface feeding that other trout do, but the brook trout will take advantage of floating food sources when available.

The modern range of the brook trout in Georgia is, in rough terms, east of Ellijay and north of an imaginary line from Dahlonega to Clarkesville. The only major point of argument with those boundaries might be the Cohutta Mountains in the watersheds of the Jacks and Conasauga rivers. There is always the possibility of some pockets of native fish being in that rugged and isolated area, but the Rich Mountain Wildlife Management Area is the farthest west that brookies have been consistently found.

During the late 1960s the native brook trout appeared to be headed for extinction in the Peach State. Due to the problems noted earlier with other invading species and degradation of the streams, the outlook was not bright. At that point the Georgia Game and Fish Commission, as it was known then, began a program to reverse the trend.

The agency first identified several streams that were ideal brook trout water but no longer contained the species. Another criterion that the creeks had to meet was that their watershed be entirely on public lands. It would be useless to reestablish the brookies in an appropriate stream unless the fisheries managers could control the surrounding woodlands to ensure the continued survival of the newly reintroduced populations.

These target streams had to have a major barrier falls on them as well to prevent rainbows and browns from migrating back into the streams after the renovation. If no existing barrier was present, then one was constructed.

Once a stream meeting all the criteria was identified, the targeted stretch of water was treated with rotenone. This poison affects only gilled life-forms, so it would eliminate competing species of fish already in the stream, but leave the food chain intact. During this poisoning process, an antidote was released into the stream below the barrier falls to protect the downstream fish populations. Once the process was completed, electroshock fish samples were taken to confirm the absence of any competing fish species. After the competitors were eliminated and the poison had dissipated, brook trout from one of the remaining stronghold streams were transplanted into the newly renovated waters. This transplanting of fish from the wild was undertaken—as opposed to using hatchery-raised brookies—to ensure survival of the true native fish stock.

To date, six streams in the Chattahoochee National Forest have undergone this treatment. On the Coleman River WMA, the Coleman River, Tate Branch, and Mill Creek have all been renovated. Tuckaluge Creek on Warwoman WMA and Dicks Creek on Lake Burton WMA have both been included in the program. The headwaters of the Chattahoochee River above Helen on the Chattahoochee WMA are the most recent waters to become a brook trout haven. The program has been a success with the exception of the Dicks Creek stocking, where it appears someone has reintroduced rainbows above the barrier. The current state record for a brook trout is 5 pounds, 10 ounces, taken by Russell Braden from Waters Creek in Lumpkin County on May 29, 1986. Because Waters Creek is a trophy stream under special regulations, the huge size of this fish is a bit misleading. Under ordinary circumstances, a brook trout of even a pound would be considered a trophy.

All of the brookies presently found in Waters Creek are from hatchery stock. The same can be said of the fish in the Toccoa River tailrace where the previous state record fish of more than 4 pounds was taken. Other large brood-stock female brook trout have been released in various Georgia waters from time to time and subsequently caught by anglers. Some impressive individuals have also turned up among the hatchery-released brook trout in the tailrace of the Chattahoochee River below Lake Lanier.

All of this is to show that brook trout that can be measured in pounds rather than inches are possible in Georgia, but they are virtually never from stream-reared native stock. Unlike the spent brood fish released directly from the hatcheries, however, the large brookies of Waters Creek, the Toccoa River, and the Chattahoochee River have lived through a number of seasons, are streamwise, and are just as difficult to hook as a native fish.

On the other waters of the state that support brook trout, the average stocked fish will rarely be larger than 12 inches, and the average for wild brookies is more like 5 inches. A wild, native brook trout of 12 inches is an impressive fish, and one reaching 14 inches would be considered a most highly prized trophy.

THE RAINBOW TROUT

As the native brook trout were pushed into the high-altitude brooklets, the vacancy in the stream's hierarchy was filled by stocked rainbow and brown trout. The more prevalent of the two is the rainbow. This hardy native of America's northwest shores has adapted well to Georgia waters, and for at least the last forty years, these trout have been stocked here. A large number of the primary trout streams of the state now support reproducing wild populations of these colorful immigrants, which spawn each year between January and June. With few exceptions they are the dominant cold-water species in most Georgia trout streams.

The coloration of rainbow trout caught in north Georgia may range from blue to green on their backs, and they will be heavily covered with black spots. In mature fish, particularly the stream-bred wild ones, a vivid red band will run down the side from gill to tail. In some cases, the area just forward of the gill plate will also show a splotch of coloration from bright red to scarlet. On the other hand, many hatchery-stocked fish will show no sign of the red hues on any portion of their bodies.

The range of rainbow trout in Georgia can be said to cover all the cold-water streams of the state. Unless special management programs have been used to keep a stream a pure brook or brown trout fishery, there will be rainbows present. These fish are the common denominator of Georgia trout angling. Part of their success, as was mentioned earlier, has to do with their ability to tolerate warmer water temperatures than either brook or brown trout, as well as being able to live in waters other than siltless, crystal clear mountain rivulets. They can withstand water temperatures in the mid-80s for short periods, though 56° to 60° F. is the ideal range.

Other factors in the rainbow's success story are its longer (7 to 11 years) life span as compared to the brook trout, and the species' preference for moving water. The age factor allows individual rainbows the chance to get larger and become the dominant fish in a pool. The affinity for swift-moving water with its broken surface acts as an added protection from predators while the fish are small. It is a safety feature lacking in the still waters of pools that are preferred by brook trout.

The current state record for rainbow trout is a 15-pounder landed by E. B. Watkins in a private pond in White County on April 18, 1985. The previous state record of more than 14 pounds was also taken from a private pond. While these records are bonafide, it is equally true that these fish reached such proportions in part because they were not subjected to the fishing pressure applied on public waters.

Before those record fish, the state mark had been held by a 12-pound rainbow that was taken from public water. This fish, however, was a brood-stock trout that had been released from one of the hatcheries into the Coosawattee River in Gilmer County. Again, the special circumstances of this catch make it unrepresentative of how large rainbow trout will usually grow in Georgia streams.

The largest rainbow caught that appears actually to have been reared in a publicly fished stream is almost as impressive as the record fish mentioned so far. The Chattahoochee River tailrace yielded a 14-pound rainbow to Nancy Crigger of Smyrna in 1987. State biologists estimated the fish to be 12 years old, which is older than the species' usual life span. Waters Creek, also, has produced rainbows in excess of 10 pounds.

In spite of these monster trout, in the average Georgia freestone trout creek, a wild 15-inch fish will earn bragging rights for most days of fishing. Fish in the 20-inch-plus class, weighing 2 to 3 pounds, will show up from these creeks each season, but in very limited numbers. Realistically speaking, anything over 18 inches from most of the area's cold-water streams would be a trophy rainbow.

Stocked rainbows will average 8 to 11 inches in most creeks, and the wild variety will run from 6 to 10 inches. Wild fish of 10 to 12 inches are possible from most of the streams, but anything larger will take patience and persistence to find and fool.

THE BROWN TROUT

The final member of Georgia's trout triumvirate is the European brown, commonly known simply as the brown trout or brownie. First introduced to America from Germany in the 1880s, other importations soon followed from England and Scotland in the same decade. Browns have been present in Georgia streams since at least the 1930s and possibly even earlier.

In appearance the brown trout lives up to its name. The overall hue of its body will be brown to golden brown, with a multitude of black spots along the sides. These spots will usually be surrounded by a lighter ring of coloration, ranging from gold to light tan. A number of red spots will also be visible on most mature fish. The belly region will be light tan to white, and stream-reared fish will often have distinct orange tips on their fins, especially from October through February as spawning takes place.

Though many creeks are home to these hearty survivors, there are only a few streams in Georgia where the brown trout is the dominant species. The upper Chattooga River above Burrells Ford in the Ellicots Rock Wilderness Area, the Chattahoochee River from Morgan Falls Dam to Peachtree Creek, and Jones Creek on the Blue Ridge WMA are all predominantly brown trout waters. In most other streams, at least a few browns will be present, and they will usually be some of the largest fish in the stream. This is especially true in marginal trout areas at lower altitudes with warmer water.

Although rainbows are more tolerant of high water temperatures, the competition from warm-water species, such as bluegill, redeye bass, and spotted bass, generally will force rainbows out of the marginal areas. The brown trout—in spite of its greater sensitivity to the temperature of its habitat (temperatures in the mid-80s are lethal, with 54° to 63° F. being ideal)—has developed a sure-fire method of overcoming the competition of other species. Once the brown has progressed beyond the juvenile state, it becomes a very effective predator and simply eliminates the competition by eating it. After attaining 12 inches in length, the brown trout's diet is made up largely of crayfish, spring lizards, and other fish.

Another reason that brownies generally compose an inordinate percentage of larger fish in a stream is that they are very adept at escaping their main predator, the trout angler. Studies on the streams of Georgia and other areas of the country have shown that the wily brown trout is much more difficult to entice than either brook or rainbow trout. In Maine it was found that five brook trout are landed for each brown caught. Likewise, in Oregon the ratio of rainbows caught to brown trout taken was four to one.

As brown trout get older their feeding patterns change, and they become even less vulnerable to the angler's offerings. The streamwise, veteran brownie who has seen four or five seasons pass is prone to live in slow pools and become a nocturnal feeder, concentrating on minnows and other denizens of the creek depths. For this reason, even when an angler fishes the pool a brown trout inhabits, the bait offered will usually be of little interest to this fish, or it will be offered at a time of day when this old-timer is simply not interested in eating. Given this scenario, it is easy to see why brown trout get larger than the other species. They generally have more time to grow before they make that fatal mistake of grabbing the wrong morsel floating down their creek.

Although the state record for brown trout in Georgia is only slightly larger than that for rainbows, the majority of trophy-proportion trout taken in the state each year are browns. This is partially due to a long life expectancy of 7 to 12 years with fish of up to 18 years old recorded. The record brownie, however, is another anomaly. On May 6, 1967, while fishing in Rock Creek on the Blue Ridge WMA, William M. Lowery hooked and landed an 18-pound, 2-ounce brown. The fish was an escaped brooder from the Chattahoochee National Fish Hatchery that lies on the creek's feeder stream, Mill Creek.

A number of creeks in the mountains have produced stream-reared fish in the 4- to 5-pound range, and a few bigger streams such as the Chattooga, Conasauga, and Jacks rivers have yielded browns of 7 to 9 pounds. The champion stream for consistently large brown trout in Georgia is the tailrace of the Chattahoochee River. While impressive, a 5-pound brown from these waters would not cause a stir among knowledgeable anglers. Fish of 6 to 10 pounds are landed each season, and several in the 13- to 16-pound category have been taken in the last decade. Undoubtedly, a new state record brown trout is living somewhere below Buford Dam, waiting to be hooked. Anyone dedicated to angling the smaller streams of the mountains must forget the gargantuan critters just described and come back down to earth, or Georgia, as the case may be. The average brown trout likely to be encountered will run from 9 to 11 inches in length, with fish of 12 to 15 inches being a real possibility on almost any stream.

As mentioned earlier, the larger fish are present, but they are also wary and hard to catch. If an angler does everything right in stalking, casting, and having the correct bait on the hook, there is still no guarantee that these browns will bite. Still, it is comforting and exciting to know that these prize fish are in the streams. That next deep, dark pool at the bend of the creek—the one with the undercut bank and tangle of tree roots—may be the home of one of those 2-foot, "magnum" brown trout that every angler envisions hanging above the fireplace.

CHAPTER TWO

The Tackle

Telling any angler what type tackle is best, or how to use it, is a sure way to start an argument. Even if two people basically agree, there would still be plenty of hairs to split. With that in mind, rather than talking in terms of what is best, let's take a look at what is possible.

Most anglers get into trout fishing the same way they begin any other type of angling. They start with the easiest method and progress to the level at which they are most comfortable and which they most enjoy. The vast majority start off by taking whatever rod and reel they have handy, tying on a small hook, adding a BB-sized splitshot weight, and tipping out the rig with a worm, a cricket, or a kernel of corn.

An example of the simple tackle necessary for trout angling is well illustrated by a haphazard fishing excursion I experienced in the mid-seventies. On a Labor Day weekend my wife, Cathi, and I decided to spend the holiday camping in the Georgia mountains. We were newlyweds of only a few months, and Cathi did not want to spend her time in camp alone, so the suggestion was made that I leave my fishing tackle at home. Being young, naive, and hardly worthy of the title of trout fisherman, I complied.

We settled into a primitive but comfortable camp on the banks of the Etowah River on the Blue Ridge WMA in Lumpkin County. From our camp I could see the stocked rainbows finning casually in the current, seemingly aware that I had no rod and thus posed no threat to them.

When Cathi lay down for a nap one afternoon, I was left to my own devices for a few hours and reverted to my baser instincts: I was no longer a husband, but a fisherman.

Scouring the trees around the campsite, I discovered a small fishhook hanging in the bark of a poplar tree. Next I scavenged a piece of monofilament line from the creek bank. These were quickly tied to a short, flexible limb from a nearby sapling. For bait I managed to catch a crawfish, whose tail section soon adorned the hook.

The perfect ending to the tale would be to explain how I landed a limit of trout for supper. Unfortunately, the truth is a bit less glamorous. I did manage to entice a couple of strikes and had one rainbow on the line, but I was unable to get it out of the water and onto the bank. The message of this story is that even the most primitive bait and tackle can catch trout, and provide an adventure in the process.

BAIT FISHING

Simple bait rigs probably account for the bulk of the trout taken in Georgia each year, as well as being the most effective tackle for hatchery-reared, freshly stocked fish. A large number of anglers never feel compelled to try any other gear and are satisfied with tossing their bait into a deep pool and waiting for the tug of a hungry trout.

At times the siren call of bait fishing will prove too strong for advanced anglers as well. On one adventure on the Cartecay River in Gilmer County, my brother-in-law, Larry Stegall, and I were fishing in the bend of the stream just below Stegall Mill in what is now the Blackberry Mountain resort. I was armed with my fly rod, while Larry was using simple bait tackle.

My first few casts with a dry fly produced a 9-inch stocked rainbow, but then the fish began to ignore my offerings. Meanwhile, Larry, who was just learning the art of trout fishing, was getting bites regularly, but he kept coming up empty-handed.

All the while I had, of course, been extolling the virtues of fly casting as compared to his bait fishing. Continuing to spout this pompous fly caster's litany—that only by fooling a trout with artificial flies can one truly lay claim to the title of "trout angler"—I kept an envious eye on the attention Larry's bait was attracting from the fish.

Finally, no longer able to stand being left out of the action, I slipped a couple of kernels of corn from Larry's bait supply when he wasn't watching. Tipping my dry fly with one of these, I tossed it into the current and, as it sank, presented it in the same way I would have a wet fly. I quickly added another rainbow to my score, while never letting up in my praise of fly-fishing.

The moral of the story is that church folks aren't the only ones who can be guilty of backsliding. A dedicated fly caster can fall victim as well.

There is not a lot of advice that can be given about bait fishing in the Georgia mountains. For stocked trout, cheese, marshmallows, kernel corn, or any natural bait like mealworms, nightcrawlers, or crickets will work. The more difficult wild trout are generally less interested in store-bought items of any kind and more attuned to those that nature concocts.

It is worth noting as well that big trout, as a general rule, are harder to fool using processed food for baits. This is due to their preferred food sources. As trout grow older, they feed heavily on crawfish, spring lizards, and minnows. Since minnows are not a legal bait in any Georgia trout streams, they are eliminated as an option. A crawfish or spring lizard can be used, but an angler using one of these is committed to catching a trophy trout because such bait is usually too large to attract strikes from smaller fish.

Probably the most glaring exception to this rule is the fishing for big rainbows that goes on in the headwaters of the lake above Morgan Falls Dam on the Chattahoochee. Anglers will drift large nightcrawlers along the bottom to fool some really hefty fish. The 14-pound, 2-ounce rainbow mentioned earlier that was taken by Nancy Crigger is a prime example of the result of this tactic.

Before moving on, a few words need to be said about artificial salmon eggs. These small rubber or plastic balls traditionally have been considered artificial baits in Georgia waters. However, the newer versions that are impregnated with natural oils have resulted in some new rulings on the matter. In 1990 the Department of Natural Resources came out with a set of criteria for determining what is an artificial bait.

If the answer is yes to any one of the four following questions, then the lure is a natural bait and *not legal* in any of the state's artificial-lure-only waters.

Can the fish eat the material?
Would it be palatable to the fish?
If the fish eat the material, can they digest it?
Does the material have any food value to the fish?

These same four factors apply as well to any additives, such as scents or fish attractants, that might be added to lures.

SPIN FISHING

While bait fishing is very effective for stocked trout and will attract wild fish, some anglers yearn for more action and participation and decide to move beyond fishing with natural bait. The next step is usually to casting small spinning lures. Again, many people will opt to continue using their medium- and light-action rods and reels, which will work fine if the angler can cast the very lightweight lures that are usually employed. Most, however, quickly turn to the excellent ultralight rods and reels that are now on the market. The reels easily handle lines as small as 2-pound test, and the shorter rods (4 1/2 to 5 1/2 feet) are better for avoiding the ever-present and often canopied foliage on the stream banks.

The lures available are almost endless in variety these days. Basic to this type of angling are the in-line spinners such as the Panther Martin, Mepps Agila, and Rooster Tail. All come in a dazzling array of colors. The brand and colors chosen tend to be more a matter of personal choice than necessity. All will take fish at times; all will be ignored by the trout at other times. Trial and error on different streams with differing water conditions is the rule of thumb for decisions about lures.

Spinners appropriate for trout usually vary in weight from the 1/8-ounce size down to as small as 1/32 ounce. Standard sizes are 1/16 or 1/24 ounce. Having made these pronouncements on size, now let me introduce my theory of big and ugly trout fishing. On certain days, you will do better to find the biggest, ugliest spinner in your tackle collection and fish with it. On several occasions, while I was being skunked or very nearly so, my fishing companions at the most novice of skill levels have caught very respectable brown trout in 14- to 15-inch lengths. They achieved this feat because they did not know that the big 1/2-ounce spinner in Day-Glo-orange and purple that they chose to chunk into the stream was totally inappropriate.

One such lesson was taught to me by State Representative Theo Titus in the spring of 1989. Theo and I, along with a motley crew of outdoor writers, ventured onto Betty Creek near Dillard to challenge some freshly stocked rainbow trout. Hailing from Thomasville in the southern reaches of the state, where a trout is known only as an entree that is infrequently found on restaurant menus, Theo chose to fish with his spinning tackle while several of us attacked the stream with fly tackle and gusto.

The overcast, rainy day produced rising waters in the creek that soon dampened our enthusiasm—at least until we heard the commotion caused by the large trout attached to the end of Theo's line. When finally landed, the rainbow was in the 17- to 18-inch class and weighed around 2 1/2 pounds. To the chagrin of the rest of us, we discovered that Theo had tied on a lead-headed jig with a curly-tail plastic crappie grub. Not your classic small-stream trout lure, but certainly effective on this occasion!

Another choice in spinning lures that will sometimes work, especially for larger fish, are any of the down-sized, ultralight versions of the popular bass lures. Many of these now come in sizes as small as 1/10 ounce and can be deadly for the older predatory trout.

FLY-FISHING

The third option for catching trout is fly-fishing. The good news is that it is a disease that can be avoided. On the other hand, the bad news is that there is generally no cure for victims of the malady. An early symptom is the desire to buy and fish with some delicate and difficult-to-handle equipment. But, if mastered, it can also be the most effective gear for fooling trout.

In spite of common misconceptions, it is not necessary to own expensive fly rods with matching high-priced reels in order to be successful. As with most types of fishing, or any other sport, the person handling the gear is the key to success or failure. Inexpensive tackle in the hands of experienced anglers will catch fish.

A frequent debate among north Georgia fly rodders centers on whether or not a short rod (7 feet or less) is desirable, perhaps even necessary, for the close quarters found on most Peach State trout streams. While short rods do provide the ability to work in cramped quarters, long rods of up to 8 1/2 feet can come in handy for reaching and dabbling a fly on the surface of fish-holding potholes that a conventional cast would never reach due to overhanging branches.

For the beginning fly-fisher, the whole debate is rather academic in nature. In the hands of a novice, both a 6-foot and a 10-foot rod will propel a high percentage of casts into the hungry boughs of Georgia's insatiable rhododendrons. The trick is to learn to use whatever length appeals to you on open pond or river water, then adapt your use of that rod to the mountain conditions. Also, since long casts are rare on these streams, the material the rod is made of is not overly important. Be it boron, graphite, or fiberglass, a rod with which an angler can accurately place a fly on the surface of a pool the size of a wash tub from a distance of 30 feet will solve most of the problem of presentation.

Just as there is no definitive answer as to what type of rod is best for north Georgia trout streams, there is no one best reel or line. The demands made on this equipment are so minimal in small-stream angling that it boils down to matters of preference. In the case of the fly line, however, a floating line is most practical. With dry flies it is a necessity and, since the water is rarely very deep, nymphs, wet flies, and streamers can be fished on such a line as well. As to whether the line should be double tapered, level, or weight forward, all will work. Anglers should choose one they prefer to cast and the one that gives the greatest control.

In the matter of terminal tackle, which is to say flies, some advice can be offered. If dry flies on the surface are the choice, the key is to use very buoyant, easily visible patterns. Classic fly-fishing literature often speaks of presenting miniscule flies on flat water and trying to achieve long, drag-free drifts down the stream. Well, don't expect that on Georgia's mountain water. Often the pocket of water that is the angler's target will be only a few feet long, and the surface will be turbulent. If the offering stays afloat for 8 to 10 seconds and can be followed visually on the rough water, that is sufficient. These trout are accustomed to seeing potential meals zipping over their heads in the fast currents. They don't hesitate or study what passes. If it looks edible, they come for it in a hurry!

All that is needed is to put something on the water that presents an outline similar to the insects the fish see regularly. These insects may be aquatic varieties such as mayflies, caddis flies, or stoneflies, which are bugs that spend their adolescence in a nymphal stage on the stream bottom. When mature, they rise to the surface to shed their husks and fly away as adults. They later return to deposit eggs on the water surface and restart the cycle.

At all levels of this cycle the insects are vulnerable and appetizing to the trout in the stream. The dry-fly angler, however, is interested in presenting an offering that looks like the adult bug that either is laying eggs or has simply fallen to the water's surface.

The other class of insects that is important to the dry-fly enthusiast is the terrestrial variety. These are land-dwelling bugs of various kinds that spend none of their life in the water, but are just unlucky enough to have fallen, jumped, or been washed into the stream. A wide array of ants, beetles, and grasshoppers fall into this category.

Almost any fly that presents a silhouette resembling that of a caddis fly with its backward-swept wing will attract Georgia trout. The caddis fly is the most common aquatic insect in the freestone streams of the mountains. Imitations of these bugs, tied with elk hair or woodchuck fur for the wings, usually work. The color of the body, however, may need to be varied to suit the fish on any given day or particular stream.

In the case of the mayflies, a commonly used and very successful fly is the Adams in both the standard pattern and the female version. The standard pattern has a body that is totally grey, while the female pattern is tied with the rear of the body being yellow. Though the trout will often readily take these flies, they are difficult for the angler to see on the surface of the water, which limits their use in the low-light conditions of shaded creek valleys.

Other standard flies for Georgia streams are the Royal Wulff and the various colors of Humpys. These flies are called attractors because they are not designed to imitate one specific type of bug. They simply present a "buggy" outline. These patterns catch a lot of Georgia trout because they are buoyant and well suited for floating on turbulent water.

Another big advantage of the Wulff pattern is that it has a white hair wing that is very visible and easy to follow on the surface. This factor is important because light conditions, even on bright summer days, are often poor in the deep, shaded creek bottoms of the mountains. Many flies that would potentially interest the fish can be extremely difficult to use because they are virtually impossible for trout anglers to see on the water's broken, sunless surface.

Water turbulence is also important in choosing the hook size for dry-fly patterns. Sizes up to No. 12 will do nicely for the range of flies large enough for both angler and fish to see on the broken surface. Here again the traditional fly-fishing adage of "smaller is better" in matching the insect hatches does not hold on Georgia streams. In fact, the theory of fishing "big and ugly" that was mentioned in the spinning-tackle discussion will hold true at times for fly casting as well.

Of course, not all insects in a stream will be on the surface of the water. Immature stages of the aquatics and drowned individuals of the terrestrial variety sink. Wet flies are designed to look like the drowned insects, while nymphs are used to imitate the insects that live on the stream's bottom in the larval stage. A variety of patterns of flies are available that suggest all of these. A few that are frequently found in the fly boxes of Georgia anglers are the wet version of the Adams and Royal Coachman (same as the Wulff, but tied with a feather wing instead of hair). Popular nymph patterns are the Pheasant Tail, Tellico, Gold-Ribbed Hare's Ear, Ted's Stonefly, and Montana Stonefly.

These subsurface offerings are often the only ones that will be effective in stocked trout streams. Freshly stocked trout are usually reluctant to take flies from the surface of the stream, but they will readily gulp down a bug tumbling along the bottom.

Finally, the fly caster can choose to use streamer flies and try to imitate the small minnows or crayfish that larger trout feed on. A couple of patterns that will work are the Muddler Minnow and the Mickey Finn.

The Muddler is the all-purpose best choice. It is tied with natural-color deer hair and can pass for a minnow or, because of its color, even a north Georgia crayfish (known locally as a crawfish or crawdad). Although the bright red and yellow pattern of the Mickey Finn resembles nothing found in a Georgia trout stream, it still attracts attention and strikes from the fish.

Obviously, there are a number of options and plenty of room for experimentation in the area of trout tackle. Regardless of the type of equipment chosen, the Peach State will have some public waters suited to that preference, and baits and lures will be mentioned only where they are particularly noted for their effectiveness on a certain piece of water.

CHAPTER THREE

The Tactics

If there is one overall key to the tactics needed to catch trout out of north Georgia's trout streams and rivers, it is the fine art of reading the stream. Specifically, we're talking about looking at a pool, a riffle, or any other part of a creek and being able to tell where the trout will be holding in that particular water. After all, you can't catch the fish if you can't find them.

This factor is crucial because the most common mistake made by novice trout anglers is that they simply fish in the wrong place. Most people learn to fish on warm-water lakes or ponds, but even for those who learned on warm-water rivers and streams, trout angling is still very different.

FEEDING HABITS

When warm-water anglers approach a trout stream, the first inclination is to cast into the deeper, calmer pools and backwaters. If bream, bass, and creek chubs are the target, then that is good water. For trout, it may or may not be a good spot. To decide the wisdom of this choice, it is important to understand the feeding habits of North Georgia trout.

The most important point to remember in regard to the habits of all species of trout is that they are very current oriented. It is the moving water that helps regulate the temperature and oxygen levels in their world, provides a measure of cover for them, and, above all, brings them the bulk of their food supply.

Much as hungry human beings hover around the kitchen at home or watch for the arrival of an ordered meal in a restaurant, trout are also attentive to the approach of food. For that reason, these fish are almost always found facing upstream into the current. This location provides the trout with the best seat in the house for spotting that next meal as it is washed downstream.

It is important to note, however, that trout rarely will be actually in the current. For most wild creatures, survival is a constant equation in which they must balance the food value of any tidbit against the amount of energy needed to obtain the morsel. If the fish has to fight the current constantly, it will burn up more body mass than it could hope to replace in most streams and eventually starve.

Trout need to find a place to hold just out of the current, while still maintaining a view of what is being carried downstream. Pockets of slower water beside or below rocks, fallen logs, or other obstructions are likely holding areas, as are seams where different speeds of water meet. Other places to look for trout are along breaks in the contour of the stream bottom, such as drops or humps. Finally, if no other features are present, the water along the bottom will virtually always be moving more slowly than at other levels of the flow and will attract the trout.

This slower water speed near the bottom of the creek is also a factor in explaining why trout are mainly subsurface feeders. Their usual proximity to the stream bed puts them in a position to spot nymphs of aquatic insects, drowned terrestrials, crawfish, or spring lizards. Studies over the years have estimated that 80 to 90 percent of the time, trout feed below the surface. The remaining time is devoted to eating bugs found floating on the surface.

The obvious conclusion to be drawn from these observations is that fishing under the surface is bound to improve the odds of hooking a trout. Somewhat different conclusions, however, have been drawn from studying samples of the stomach contents of fish. Evidence from one such study, conducted on Convict Creek in California, shows that, though the trout were spending less time feeding on the surface, they were getting almost a third of their food supply there. In other words, when food does appear on the surface, trout can obtain larger quantities while expending less time in the effort. The only reason they do not feed more often on the surface is that food is not always available there.

My own on-stream observations point to much the same conclusion. When fish are actively feeding they will strike lures or flies whether presented on top of or beneath the water, but *in periods of slack feeding* they are more likely to go for a dry fly presented on the surface, simply because it represents easy pickings.

One final point needs to be made about the feeding habits of Georgia trout before going on to take a look at specific stream features. In the traditional sense, insect hatches are fairly rare events on our state's freestone streams. By freestone, we mean streams that are basically formed from the runoff of rainwater and from small mountain springs. These creeks tend to have steep gradients and swift currents. Neither is very conducive to insect hatches.

These characteristics are very different from those of the limestone spring creeks in the north and west that are much praised in fishing literature. Those streams are fed from underground springs filtering out of porous limestone lowlands and generally have very minor gradients, plus very nutrient-rich waters. The resulting aquatic insect populations are quite large and often predictable as to when and where they will go through their mating, egg-laying, and hatching activities. These activities determine when the trout will go on feeding binges and become easier prey to anglers.

On our Peach State streams, true hatches are rare and very unpredictable. The nutrient-poor waters of our tumbling freestone streams do provide a wide variety of aquatic insects, but none that is dominant at any given time. It is simply a constant smorgasbord of buggy appetizers, entrees, and desserts for the trout.

The nearest thing to a predictable hatching cycle that we have in the Georgia highlands is what Don Pfitzer calls the "terrestrial hatch." Now retired from the U.S. Fish and Wildlife Service, Don spent many years in the southeastern states and was active in restoring the area's trout population.

According to his observations, the constant supply of terrestrial insects blown into the streams amounts to a "hatch" in that it is a food source on which the trout depend. Inspections of the stomachs of Georgia trout reveal that the most commonly found insect, or food form of any kind, is, in fact, the common black ant.

READING A STREAM

Trout feeding habits naturally dictate feeding habitats. Observation and experience reveal just how trout will be found around the various stream features prevalent in Georgia.

POOLS

Undoubtedly, the most frequently fished areas of any trout stream in our highlands are the slow, deep, and calm pools. These are fishing destinations that are just too tempting to be ignored.

Such "honey holes" especially attract freshly stocked, hatchery-reared fish and will also hold wild fish on streams where they are present, particularly brook and brown trout. But all wild fish will be very skittish and easily spooked in such water. Thus the pool offers its bonanza of stockers to the beginner or bait angler, while posing interesting problems for the old hand looking for a challenge.

Pools can be broken down into three distinct parts for the purpose of discussing fishing for trout in them. Beginning at the lower end and moving upstream these are the lip, the body, and the head of the pool.

In general, it is safe to say that the lip of the average pool on a North Georgia trout stream is by far the area of water most often overlooked. The lip is the downstream end of the pool where the water exits, and many people new to trout fishing do not realize that fish will hold in this part of the pool. What the experienced angler realizes, however, is that the lip is a very difficult place to fish.

Regardless of the reasons for this lack of attention, lip areas are excellent holding water, especially for wild trout. The fish position themselves at the lip to take advantage of the funnel effect found there in most pools. The flow narrows to an inverted pyramid shape as it approaches the end of the calm, slower body of the pool, and all of the floating and submerged food that is being swept along converges at the bottom of this pyramid. A trout stationed there gets an excellent view of everything coming out of the pool and can feed at its leisure. This lie is often a favorite with the dominant and largest fish in a pool.

Because it is a good position from which to see the entire pool, the lip also offers a measure of safety to the trout. The fish is very easy to spook if an angler approaches the water from either the head or side of the pool. Anglers most often become aware of lip-hanging trout when they spot the fish scurrying upstream in a panicked rush, after having seen their human adversaries' movements.

Probably the easiest method of fishing a lip area is to move upstream toward the pool casting a small spinner. This approach allows the angler to stay far enough downstream to avoid detection and still have the casting range to put the lure above the fish and retrieve it back down to the lip.

The main problem with this tactic is that the line will be stretched directly over the fish and can alert it to the presence of something unusual in the neighborhood. This is especially likely if the line is allowed to fall slack on the surface when the lure strikes the water. For that matter, the splash of the spinner landing can have the same effect.

The lip is almost impossible to fish successfully with bait. Normally bait anglers, approaching from above the pool, try to put their offering into the flow and let it drift down to the unsuspecting quarry. This is a very difficult maneuver when a wary fish is looking upstream through the pool's relatively calm water. In fact, many bait casters never even attempt to catch the lip-hanging trout, opting instead for the easier-to-take fish in the main body of the pool.

The fly caster also faces some challenging conditions in fishing a lip area. The upstream approach (i.e., moving toward the pool from downstream) is very difficult because fly-casting tackle puts an even more visible type of line over the fish's head. Although the almost weightless fly can be landed on the surface without much disturbance, the current flowing directly back toward the angler quickly tends to put drag on the fly and give it an unnatural look as it is dragged downstream.

Both the bait angler and the fly caster must practice some of the stalking arts usually associated with hunting in order to have a shot at a lip-hanger. Using any cover that is available in the form of trees or boulders, the approach should be from the side of the pool, slightly upstream of the lip. Of course, pools will not always have fish hanging on the lip, since they will only be there when feeding. Thus it is a hit-or-miss proposition to approach every pool in this stalking fashion. Most anglers seem to lack the patience for this tactic, which is another reason few lip-hanging trout are caught.

Just upstream from the lip is the main body of the pool. It is usually the deepest area of the flow and also has the calmest surface. Fortunately for the angler, the trout feel a bit more secure in this deeper water and are not as spooky as when they are in the shallower flow at the lip. As a result, they are less prone to panic at even the slightest of movements perceived upstream.

These pool areas are best for fishing bait, spinners, streamers, weighted nymphs, and wet flies, all of which can get down deep to where the fish lie. Surface-fished flies do not usually produce as well unless the trout are already actively feeding on top. Best results come from casting around logs, brush, large rocks, breaks in the contour of the bottom and undercut banks.

Finally, the easiest portion of a pool to fish is its head. This is where the chute of water enters the upstream end of the pool. The fish like to hold here because it offers them the first view of food coming into their domain. The broken surface also offers a measure of protection from overhead predators.

Both of these factors can be turned to the angler's advantage. Close approach from any direction is usually possible, but especially from downstream. Bait, spinners, or flies worked in or around the chute area will attract hungry fish.

Bait offerings should be tossed into the head of the chute and fished on a tight line as they tumble down the flow. Spinners can be run across and down the current, as can wet flies, nymphs, or streamers. In the case of dry flies, they can be floated down the main flow of the chute if the water is not too choppy. If it is, then aim for the crease of calmer water that will almost always be found just on the edge of the chute on either side.

Also not to be overlooked by the dry-fly angler are the eddies formed at the very head of the chute. These small pockets of water that swirl back on the main flow will often allow a surface fly to float in circles for up to 20 or 30 seconds without drowning. By then, a fish under the chute may have spotted it and come up for a snack with a splashy rise.

POCKETS AND EDDIES

Pockets and eddies are also found in other areas of the stream, and anglers who learn to read these features will discover that they are favorite lies for the trout. Pockets and eddies actually form miniature pools that will be situated in the churning or gurgling waters of the shoal and riffle areas. The chute will often cover the entire surface of these mini-pools. Quite often an obstruction in the flow such as a rock jutting up from the bottom will cause these pockets of slightly calmer water. Trout love them, and many anglers fail to notice them.

A good pocket will seldom hold more than one or two fish, but pockets will be scattered along the entire length of the creek. Additionally, the surrounding rough water makes the pockets easy to approach without spooking the trout. Rainbows are particularly fond of this type of water and will be found in pockets more often than either brook or brown trout.

The broken surfaces of pockets and eddies make them a particularly good choice for fishing on bright, sunny days. The light penetrates such waters much less than calm pools. Quite often during the middle of a bright day this will be the very best location for taking fish.

Regardless of the conditions, fishing pocket water requires many of the same skills as those employed on pools, only on a smaller scale. The casts will be shorter, the retrieve not as long, the drift of the fly briefer, but the size of the fish will not necessarily be smaller. Surprisingly tiny pockets can hold some hefty trout on most streams.

RETRIEVING UPSTREAM

Finally, I want to talk a little bit about one of the myths that has grown up around the art of fishing small streams in North Georgia. Specifically, I mean the idea that retrieving a spinner or fly upstream against the current will not take fish. Like any other rule, there will always be exceptions. Generally speaking, letting a bait or lure flow with the current will look most natural and take more fish, but there are times when other tactics are needed.

On one particular trip to Nimblewill Creek on the Blue Ridge WMA, the fish had seemingly lost all interest in my spinners early in the afternoon after a successful morning of casting. On a whim I tossed my Rooster Tail downstream into a pocket and pulled it back upstream virtually on the surface. A stocked rainbow rushed up to take it. Over the next hour or so the sequence was repeated a dozen times successfully.

This phenomenon is not confined to spin fishing. A good example of the same results when fly-fishing occurred on the trip to Betty Creek that I mentioned in an earlier chapter. With the inclement weather we were enduring that day, the creek was rising and beginning to become stained. I began the day by casting dry flies. Soon I had tried every pattern I carried without success. As the day progressed and the conditions deteriorated, I tried wet flies, nymphs, and streamers. Nothing was working.

Of course, I presented each of these types of flies in the prescribed, traditional manner. Dries were cast upstream and floated down on the current; wets and nymphs were fished down and across the current, as were the streamers. Then, about the time that I was convinced the pursuit was hopeless, Don Pfitzer came into view, fishing downstream toward me.

After I had finished bemoaning our fate and proposing that we abandon the fishing and get in out of the constant drizzle, Don told me he had been catching trout. I could hardly believe his explanation that he had been fishing a rubber-legged, black-bodied wet fly he calls a "bream buster" by casting it downstream and then retrieving it on the surface against the current. As the bug was pulled upstream, it created a "V" on the surface.

Had Don not been someone whose fishing expertise I respected, I would have written off this unlikely story as an attempt to make me the victim of a practical joke. Tying one of these panfish flies on my line, however, I threw it downstream and began stripping in line. On the first cast, a rainbow of 9 inches came up and pounded the fly. A couple of casts later a 14-inch stocker gave a similar performance.

Under the extremely adverse angling conditions of the day, Don and I caught a number of trout between us with this unorthodox tactic. I have always wondered how in the world an experienced fly-fisherman like Pfitzer stumbled onto the idea of casting a panfish fly the wrong direction on the stream. We broke most of the rules of fly casting, but we caught trout on Betty Creek that day.

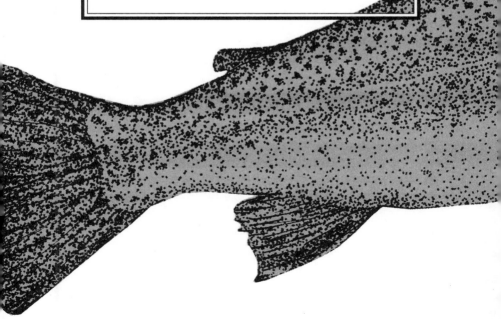

PART 2

Tailraces and Big Waters

To put tackle and tactics to use, I want to turn next to the heart of this guide, a description of Georgia's trout waters. As discussed earlier, the main criteria for covering sites in this book will be the size of the streams and public access to them. For tailraces and large streams the size factor will not play a part, but the access will.

It is important to remember that, in Georgia, the permission of a landowner is required in order to fish on private property. Under state law, land holders who have title to the shoreline of a stream also own the stream to the middle of its course. If they own both shores of the stream, then they also have title to the complete stream bed.

The only exceptions to this rule are waters that have been declared navigable by the Army Corps of Engineers or that have been recognized by state courts as "traditionally navigable." This latter definition includes recreational floating by canoes and sport-fishing boats, and applies on the tailrace waters that will be discussed.

Even in the case of the tailraces, when fishing from a boat or using a float-tube, it is a good rule of thumb to stay on or in the water unless consent to go ashore has been obtained from the landowner or the streamside property is clearly marked as publicly owned.

Let's begin by taking a look at the three tailraces in the state and the fishing each supports. These streams are the Chattahoochee River below Buford Dam at Lake Sidney Lanier, the Toccoa River below Lake Blue Ridge, and the Savannah River below the dam at Lake Hartwell.

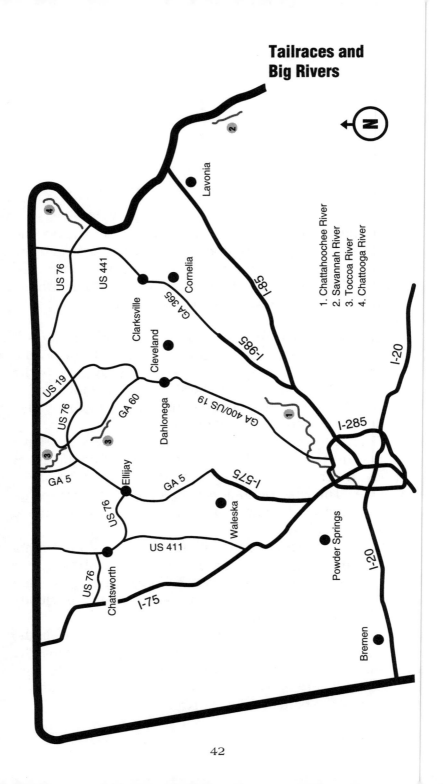

Tailraces and Big Rivers

1. Chattahoochee River
2. Savannah River
3. Toccoa River
4. Chattooga River

By tailraces, we are talking about areas downstream from major hydroelectric dams. These rivers are fed by the icy waters coming through the dams from the bottom of the impounded reservoirs, making it possible for trout to survive in these rivers. Without the releases of cold water, all three streams would be warm-water fisheries.

Some shared characteristics are worth mentioning about these fisheries. They are all big waters, which is to say they are several hundred feet wide, have some deep areas, and are subject to very changeable flows. When water is released from the dams, the placid surfaces can quickly become rushing torrents that are unfishable.

Even more important, these waters can become downright dangerous. Several deaths have occurred over the past several fishing seasons, particularly on the Chattahoochee, when anglers did not pay close enough attention to the level of the water in the river. The rising flood resulting from the opening of the power-generation gates at the dam have swept wading anglers away and swamped small fishing boats.

Below these dams, sirens have been installed along the river that sound when a release is imminent, and on the Chattahoochee a low-powered radio transmitter broadcasts a release schedule. As helpful as these are, they are not a substitute for people staying alert to their surroundings. Always check the recorded release schedules that are provided for each dam. The telephone numbers for these can be obtained by calling directory assistance in the dam's local phone exchange.

The primary safety measure is always to be aware of the water level when entering the river and to watch for any hint of rapid changes. If the water level starts to rise, *get out immediately.*

In regard to fishing tailrace waters, these streams are not primary trout water. All receive heavy doses of hatchery-raised trout, but the streams are so large that many fish will carry over from year to year. For that reason, the trout are almost a hybrid between the wild and hatchery fish. They may not be as wary as a stream-raised trout, but they are definitely more challenging than freshly planted stockers.

Because of the size of these rivers, float fishing is the predominant method of covering these waters. Although there are some wadable areas on two of the three tailraces, floating will open much more water to angling. Small johnboats, canoes, and float-tubes are the vehicles most often employed for floating, but on the Chattahoochee you may even see bass boats on the stream.

CHAPTER FOUR

Chattahoochee River

The portion of the Chattahoochee that makes up the tailrace fishery is from the foot of Lake Lanier's Buford Dam down to Atlanta. Altogether, this stretch contains about 46 miles of water, reaching to the mouth of Peachtree Creek in northwest Atlanta.

The vast majority of trout in the river are put-and-take stockers. Although there have been hints that some fish may actually spawn, the percentage would be so low as to be negligible to the fishery. Up to 200,000 catchable-sized fish are released in this flow each year. This heavy stocking is due in part to the presence of a state trout hatchery on the upper reaches of the tailrace.

As noted, unlike the stockers in the mountain streams, Chattahoochee trout are likely to carry over to the following years if they are not caught immediately. They will also attain at least some of the characteristics of wild fish in that they become wary and more selective regarding what they eat.

Brook, rainbow, and brown trout are all present in the Chattahoochee tailrace, with rainbows being dominant in most of the area. Browns make up the bulk of the larger fish, especially in the lower stretches of the trout water. These big browns are also the reason that the Chattahoochee is the premier stream in the Peach State for trophy-sized trout.

The ideal time for fishing this river, which the locals often refer to as the "Hooch," is on low water when no power generation is taking place at Buford Dam. Conversely, during generation periods the river runs high and muddy and is unfishable.

For the trout angler, there are four discernible parts of the Chattahoochee tailrace, each of which has a character of its own. The sections are from Buford Dam down to the GA 20 bridge, GA 20 to GA 141 at Medlock Bridge, GA 141 downstream to GA 9, and, finally, GA 9 to Peachtree Creek.

FROM BUFORD DAM TO THE GA 20 BRIDGE
SIZE: *Large*
ACCESS: *Easy*
SPECIES: *Stocked brook, brown, and rainbow trout*

The upper section of the Chattahoochee, beginning at the foot of Buford Dam, may be the best area to catch trout from the river, but it is not necessarily the best or easiest portion to fish. One reason that the fishing is often good on this roughly 2.5-mile stretch is that the stocked trout are usually hungry.

Because of the scouring effect of the releases of water for power generation at the dam, the bottom of the river here is sandy and barren of aquatic weeds and insect life. This lack of natural foods in the stream results in fierce competition for food among the stocked trout and a willingness to strike a wide variety of artificial and natural baits.

Also associated with these power generation releases, of course, are very substantial and dangerous variations in water level. A few years back, a fishing buddy and I decided to take a weekend and float fish the entire tailrace from the dam down to Atlanta. For this adventure we chose a 12-foot johnboat to provide the best possible fishing platform. Late on a Friday afternoon in April we arrived in the National Park

Service access at the foot of the dam. We had timed our arrival to coincide with the time the generators were to be shut down for the weekend. We left our boat at the water's edge and returned our truck to the parking area.

When we got back to the boat with the first load of fishing and camping gear, we discovered that the water was now a good 10 feet from the boat and still falling. The park is one of the few places on the upper river that offers a gently inclined approach, so this represented about a 2-foot drop in the water level. We dragged the partially loaded boat back to the water's edge and went for another load of gear.

This scene of loading gear and dragging the boat back to the water's brink was repeated several times, as the river fell at least 7 to 8 feet in just a few minutes. In all we had to drag the increasingly heavy boat a good 30 feet in pursuit of the river. Fluctuations are obviously at their most exaggerated extremes here at the source of the changing water level.

Another result of the scouring of the stream's course by the rising waters is the carving out of high steep banks that make the river difficult to approach in much of its upper reaches. This characteristic also became a factor in our ill-conceived weekend on the Hooch.

Once we had launched our boat, we spent a couple of hours casting for trout that we intended to have for dinner later in the evening. Unfortunately, the fish did not cooperate, and one lone 10-inch brown ended up on the stringer. With nightfall fast approaching we began looking for a place to beach the boat and make a camp.

After looking fruitlessly along the steep shoreline for almost an hour, our search was becoming a frantic attempt to get off the water before nightfall. Finally, out of desperation, we tied the boat to a fallen tree and laboriously carried our gear up the bank to a meadow above. In our haste to make camp, we forgot about our lone trout.

During the night, we heard the boat banging against the tree, but it was first light before we realized the significance of those sounds. We found the boat hanging at a steep angle, still moored to the tree but completely out of the water, as was the stringer holding the fish. I can say from experience that the changes in the water level need to be carefully planned for when you fish on the Chattahoochee.

Although there is some wadable water at Bowman Island Shoals just downstream and within sight of the dam, extreme care is necessary in this area. Anglers have been swept away and some even drowned by the rising, icy water when the gates at the dam are opened. Fishing from a boat is a better option, but the rising flood is also capable of swamping a boat that is anchored or poorly handled. The watchword on the upper Chattahoochee tailrace is always "Caution."

For the careful angler, the rewards can be great on the upper tailrace. Stocked rainbow trout are abundant and usually hungry when the water is low. Fish up to 15 inches are common, and an occasional 20-incher will show up. Most of the time fishing pressure is only medium on this part of the river.

One lure of significance to note for use on this upper section is the Little Cleo spoon in the 1/8-ounce size. On certain days, the fish in this section will turn up their collective noses at just about any other lure. Many veteran anglers swear the only proper lure color for use here is gold.

Access points for this first section are at the park below Buford Dam and at GA 20. Be aware that a guard rail has been installed at the GA 20 crossing, severely limiting the parking space available.

FROM GA 20 TO GA 141

    SIZE: *Large*
    ACCESS: *Easy*
    SPECIES: *Stocked brook, brown, and rainbow trout*
    SPECIAL REGULATIONS: *Artificial lures only*

Moving downstream, the next section of water encountered is the regulated portion of the river between highways 20 and 141. Ending at Medlock Bridge, this long stretch of more than 16 miles is limited to artificial lures only and is probably the most heavily fished section of the river.

On this portion of the tailrace there is some wadable water at Fish Weir Shoals just below GA 20, and some of the main flow of the river is also wadable farther downstream. Rather than rocky shoals, however, this shallow water comes in the form of submerged sandbars out in the center of the river. These allow the angler to wade and fish back toward either shore, where there will be a trough of deeper water along the bank.

Though wading allows more thorough coverage of the water, it is a good idea to combine wading with floating. Even on this part of the river, as much as a dozen miles downstream from Buford Dam, the waters can rise quickly when power generation begins.

On one excursion near Rodgers Bridge, a companion and I had moored a johnboat in the center of the river and were wading the bars. Fortunately, we had the good sense to mentally mark the water level at the time we began casting. Later, we noticed the flow was creeping up just a bit on the streamside feature we had chosen for a makeshift water gauge. We quickly waded back to the boat and were soon glad we made that decision. Within another 15 minutes the river went up about 3 feet, making it hard even to maneuver the boat back to our take-out point a few hundred yards downstream. Again, caution is necessary at all times on the Chattahoochee, particularly when wading.

Fishing from a johnboat, canoe, or float-tube is the most popular way to approach this second section of the Chattahoochee. Floating still offers a shot at most of the trout's preferred hiding places in the brush and logjams that lie close to the shore.

All three trout species will usually be present, with the abundance of each dictated by the latest stocking pattern. Most fish will be in the 9- to 14-inch class, but bruisers of up to 6 or 8 pounds are possible. These bigger fish will usually be brown trout, but some respectable rainbows also show up.

Good lure choices for spin fishing this section are the Little Cleo, in-line spinners, and small Rapala topwater minnows. During years when Japanese beetles are present, any fly that imitates them probably will provoke some vicious strikes.

My first fishing trip to this part of the river was on a Fourth of July weekend on which I fished a full eight-hour day without encountering any anglers except the members of my own party. That, however, was back in the late seventies, and things have changed in the ensuing years. Now the fishing pressure along this whole section will be medium to heavy on any weekend of the season. In areas immediately around access points, the river will often appear to be hosting a regatta of miscellaneous watercraft, all containing anglers.

There are a number of access points along the artificial-only section of the Hooch's tailrace. Beginning upstream, GA 20, Settles Bridge, McGinnis Ferry, Abbotts Bridge (GA 120), McClure Bridge and Medlock Bridge (GA 141) all offer varying degrees of access. The parks at Abbotts and Medlock bridges both have improved boat ramps.

FROM GA 141 TO GA 9

> SIZE: *Large*
> ACCESS: *Easy*
> SPECIES: *Stocked brook, brown, and rainbow trout*

The third section of the Chattahoochee tailrace, moving downriver, consists of the flow from Medlock Bridge to GA 9 (Roswell Road) bridge near Roswell. This area is again open to all types of angling, including natural baits. It is also best suited for fishing with the aid of a boat or float-tube.

There can be little doubt that this is the part of the tailrace in which to find a really big trout. Browns in the 14- to 16-pound range (that's pounds, not inches) have been taken, as have rainbows of up to 14 pounds.

Another encouraging feature of this section is that the scouring effect of water-release periods dissipates to the point that some aquatic insect life begins to appear. This is particularly true around Old Jones Bridge Shoals and at Island Ford Shoals. The former hosts sporadic hatches of caddis flies during the spring and summer months. During this activity, caddis imitations can provide some fast fly rod action.

The portion of the river just at the end of Island Ford Shoals and going into the headwaters of Bull Sluice Lake (also called Lake Roswell or Morgan Falls Lake on some maps) above Georgia Power's small electric generation facility at Morgan Falls is another of interest to trophy trout anglers. Nightcrawlers dragged slowly through holes on the bottom or minnow-imitating, topwater jerk baits have both produced some fish in the 6- to 9-pound range along this part of the tailrace.

Overall this segment is less crowded than the portion lying upstream. For the most part there is medium fishing pressure, with the exception, however, of the Old Jones Bridge Park area, where it is heavy most of the time.

The access points for this stretch are at Abbotts Bridge, Old Jones Bridge Park, Holcomb Bridge, Island Ford, Vickery Creek (at the head of Bull Sluice Lake), and a number of spots along Azalea Drive and Willeo Road on the northwest side of the lake. There is no serviceable bridge at Old Jones Bridge, but there are parks on either side of the river and a boat ramp on the Fulton County (west) side.

FROM GA 9 TO PEACHTREE CREEK
SIZE: *Large*
ACCESS: *Easy*
SPECIES: *Stocked brown trout*
SPECIAL REGULATIONS: *Open year-round*

The final segment of trout water descending the Hooch's tailrace is from GA 9 bridge to the mouth of Peachtree Creek. The 4 miles of water from GA 9 to Morgan Falls Dam is, however, in Bull Sluice Lake, so the stream fishing on this section actually begins at Morgan Falls. For several years, due to a combination of several factors, this area was arguably the premier fly fishing water in Georgia.

To begin with, this section contains wadable water at Cochran, Devils Race Course, Thornton, and Long Island shoals. Also, only fingerling brown trout are stocked on a put-grow-and-take basis, providing a sound footing for the stream's former reputation. Cap these factors off with an abundance of aquatic weeds and the accompanying insect life and here are the makings of a first-rate fly-fishing resource. Finally, add in the extra bonus of having the waters open to fishing 12 months of the year, and the combination sounds unbeatable.

Such was the case through the mid-1980s, with reliable late-afternoon hatches, particularly of Light Cahills, provoking plenty of surface feeding by hefty-bodied browns during the spring. It was often possible to take fish in the 13- to 14-inch range on flies of No. 12 and smaller. All through the summer, hatches of midges would also appear, calling for the presentation of Blue-winged Olives or Adams patterns in size No. 20.

When the fish were on one of these surface-feeding binges, they would ignore everything except the insects, which could drive spin and bait anglers to distraction. On several occasions while wading in the Chattahoochee's Long Island area, I have taken surface-feeding browns on flies fished right under the bow of canoes in which frustrated casters had thrown everything except their paddles at the fish. It was truly exciting and satisfying fishing for the fly caster.

Unfortunately, the drought conditions and resulting restricted flows of the late eighties, plus silting from river corridor development, greatly reduced the angling appeal of this section. More recently there have been some signs of a possible comeback of the fishery, but the jury is still out.

Boating, wading, or tubing are all viable methods of fishing this last segment of the tailrace. Fishing pressure will ordinarily be only light to medium. Below US 41, down to Peachtree Creek, the land along both shores is privately owned. There is no access, and fishing pressure is virtually nonexistent.

Another consideration to take into account is the heavy rafting pressure the Chattahoochee gets from Johnsons Ferry to US 41 on every summer weekend. After about 10 A.M. it is almost impossible to fish because of the hundreds of rafts on the river.

Access points to the lower tailrace are at Morgan Falls Dam off Roswell Road, Johnsons Ferry Road in Cobb County, Cochran Shoals along both shores upstream of I-285 and at US 41. It is also possible to approach the river at the mouth of Peachtree Creek through the Atlanta Waterworks facilities at the Standing Peachtree historic site. This stretch of the river from Roswell Road bridge (GA 9) at the headwaters of Bull Sluice Lake is open to fishing year round.

A map of the Chattahoochee showing all of the access points is available from the National Park Service by contacting the Office of the Superintendent of the Chattahoochee River National Recreation Area, 1978 Island Ford Parkway, Dunwoody, Georgia 30350.

CHAPTER FIVE

Savannah River

SIZE: *Large*
ACCESS: *Easy*
SPECIES: *Stocked brook, brown, and rainbow trout*
SPECIAL REGULATIONS: *Open year-round*

The second of Georgia's three tailraces that hold trout is found below Lake Hartwell on the Savannah River. This fishery is located in the northeast corner of the state on the border with South Carolina.

Originally, there were 14 miles of trout water on the Savannah, but with the downstream impoundment of Lake Russell in 1982, the river has been reduced to a shadow of its former self. Today it is more like a lake fishery than a stream resource. The headwaters of Lake Russell begin virtually at the foot of Hartwell Dam.

As is so often the case, the need for more electric power to feed industries and towns won out over the need to preserve free-flowing river waters. From the standpoint of the trout angler it was a terrible loss.

The river is open to year-round fishing. Stocking of trout is done at the foot of the dam and is composed of 85 percent rainbows, 15 percent brown trout, and occasional releases of a limited number of brookies. The larger fish that carry over are most often taken farther downstream, away from the dam. Trout of up to 10 pounds have been caught on the Savannah tailrace, and fish of 20 inches are taken every year. Most fall victim to natural baits or spinners cast into the flow during low water levels.

All of the fishing on the portion of the river immediately below the dam is from the bank. Signs are posted prohibiting wading and warning of the danger of even standing on exposed streamside rocks during low flows. All boat access is from the ramps in the upper end of Lake Russell, and even this is limited by a barrier cable that denies upstream movement to the last several hundred yards below Hartwell Dam. There is a siren that sounds just before water releases begin as the turbines are turned on at the dam, so be alert for its whine.

For those still interested in fishing what is left of the Savannah's trout water, small fishing platforms are provided on both the Georgia and South Carolina sides of the river below the dam. Fishing pressure is generally light to medium on the Savannah.

To reach the park at the foot of the dam below Lake Hartwell, look for the signs on US 29 where it crosses the river just downstream of Hartwell Dam.

CHAPTER SIX

Toccoa River

SIZE: *Large*
ACCESS: *Easy*
SPECIES: *Stocked brook, brown, and rainbow trout*
SPECIAL REGULATIONS: *Open year-round*

The final tailrace that will be covered is the Toccoa River below Blue Ridge Lake in northwest Georgia. It flows north for roughly 20 miles through Fannin County from Blue Ridge Dam at the town of Blue Ridge to McCaysville on the Tennessee border. Many knowledgeable trout anglers now consider it to be the best destination for trout fishing in the Peach State. That estimation is based on the large numbers of healthy trout in the stream, their aggressive feeding habits, the reliability of the fishery, and the relatively low fishing pressure in comparision to the Chattahoochee.

As a general rule of thumb, the best fishing on the Toccoa occurs during periods of falling water when the generators at the dam have just fallen silent. Once the water level hits its lowest point, the fishing usually dies. The only exception is the fishing along the walls on the lower side of the dam itself, where bait anglers continue to catch fish during low water. In many cases, this is sight fishing, casting to trout that are visible in the clear waters along the concrete walls.

Anglers who fish this tailrace on a regular basis have discovered that by pacing the falling waters and staying just ahead of the ebbing flow, good fishing can be enjoyed over a period of several hours and several miles of the Toccoa. It takes a while to get the knack of this type of fishing, but it can pay handsome dividends in feisty rainbow trout when mastered. Although one can hopscotch along the shore to stay ahead of the receding water, floating with it is much easier.

When the fish are active in the Toccoa tailrace, they will take most of the baits, spinning lures, and flies that work on other Georgia streams. For the fly angler, stonefly nymphs will be most productive early in the year, with dry-fly fishing using caddis or mayfly patterns picking up in the summer, especially around dusk.

All of the trout below Blue Ridge Dam are stockers, since any natural reproduction in the tailrace is negligible. The bulk of the fish will be rainbow trout, with some brookies and browns. In fact, a one-time state record brook trout of more than 4 pounds was landed on the Toccoa tailrace. The average fish, however, will be in the range of 9 to 12 inches.

The long, deep pools broken by occasional shoals make the Toccoa ideal water for float-fishing, which is the method that accounts for most of the fishing pressure on the tailrace. That pressure will generally be light to moderate.

For the visiting angler, access to the river is the major problem encountered. There is a park at the foot of the dam, plus some streamside approaches further downstream. These are found mostly at bridge crossings in Mineral Bluff and McCaysville, where some limited wading water is available. Another bonus that makes the Toccoa tailrace an attractive angling option is that the river is open to year-round trout fishing over its entire length below Blue Ridge Dam.

The generating schedule of Blue Ridge Dam is available from the office of the Tennessee Valley Authority (TVA) in Knoxville, Tennessee. TVA provides information of this type for all of their projects in the Tennessee River drainage.

CHAPTER SEVEN

Upper Toccoa River

SIZE: *Large*
ACCESS: *Easy*
SPECIES: *Stocked brook trout, stocked and wild brown and rainbow trout*
SPECIAL REGULATIONS: *Open year-round*

The portion of the Toccoa River that lies upstream of Blue Ridge Lake is a large stream, but not a tailrace. The river flows for more than 40 miles through Fannin and Union counties in the north-central part of the state. Like the tailrace below Blue Ridge, the upper reaches of the river are also open to trout angling all 12 months of the year. The fish in the upper Toccoa are a mixture of both stocked trout and stream-bred natives, with rainbows again being the predominant fish.

Although a great deal of the river bank is in private hands, the Toccoa is being included because it is such big water (mostly in the 50- to 100-foot range) and there is access at bridges and on patches of National Forest land along its length. Most of the headwaters of the river near Suches are privately held and not open to public fishing. From the US Forest Service campground at Deep Hole downstream to Lake

Blue Ridge, however, portions of the river are available to the visiting angler.

This area is virtually all wadable and is heavily stocked with trout. The best fishing will be found anywhere that the current sweeps the bank, and around all in-stream breaks in the flow. Early in the year earthworms are a favored bait among the regulars on the Toccoa, but by midsummer grasshoppers will work better because some of the river runs through open pasture lands, which are fertile breeding grounds for these insects. Many of them find their way into the river by accident, and the trout have become accustomed to feeding on them.

For spinning tackle, Rapalas or other small, topwater, minnow-imitating lures work well. During clear-water conditions a rainbow trout pattern is a good choice, while stained water calls for a silver-and-black color combination. Under these latter water conditions, spinners with gold blades will also usually produce more fish.

Although some weekends may find the river crowded, overall the fishing pressure would rate as only moderate. One access point for this upper part of the river is at the Deep Hole Forest Service campground just off GA 60. Other approaches are located on Newport Road just upstream from the crossroads known as Dial and along the stretch of river immediately above Shallowford Bridge.

From Shallowford Bridge down to Blue Ridge Lake the character of the river changes slightly. Instead of open pastures, most of the land along the river is heavily wooded as the stream flows through a mixture of Forest Service lands and private land dotted with mountain cabins. This area also becomes marginal trout water, particularly in the summer months when the sun heats the water. Angling pressure on the portion of the river just above Blue Ridge Lake is only light to medium.

Access is available downstream from Shallowford Bridge at several points along Aska Road. There are also a number of dirt roads that lead to the river off Aska Road and approach the river from its southwest side. Several of these are on Forest Service land, and primitive campsites are obvious along the roads near the riverbank.

CHAPTER EIGHT

Chattooga River

SIZE: *Large*
ACCESS: *Easy to moderate*
SPECIES: *Stocked brook and rainbow trout,*
 stocked and wild brown trout
SPECIAL REGULATIONS: *Open year-round*

The extreme northeast corner of Georgia is the setting for the final big-water stream that will be covered. The Chattooga River has several appealing qualities. To begin with, it is a large stream, and its entire length is open to public use. This is a result of the river being on US Forest Service land and being included in the federal Wild and Scenic River System. Although the Chattooga does not flow through any WMAs, the corridor along both sides is protected from development by federal regulations. Also, the entire length of the river is open to year-round angling for trout.

The most northerly access point in Georgia for the Chattooga is at Burrells Ford, roughly 4.5 miles south of the border with North Carolina. This crossing also makes a good breaking point for discussing the trout fishing on the stream.

Downstream from the bridge at Burrells Ford the river is up to 100 feet wide and is heavily stocked with trout. Most of the stockers are rainbows, but a sprinkling of browns and brookies are also released.

This lower part of the river was made famous as the site of filming for the movie *Deliverance* during the early 1970s. It is just as inaccessible today as it was when the film crews were forced to float all their camera equipment downstream on rafts. For that reason, some of the trout stocking on this portion of the flow is done by helicopter.

The river is classified as trout water all the way down to its junction with the Tallulah River at Lake Tugalo. The lower portions of this flow, below the GA 28 bridge, are marginal, however, and contain few trout.

A word about the creeks that feed the Chattooga is in order. On the Georgia side, the West Fork of the Chattooga is the main tributary stream and is also open to fishing year-round. Access to this feeder is fairly good from GA 28 as the West Fork approaches the main flow of the river and from the Forest Service road (FS 86) that runs off of GA 28 and follows the stream up near its headwaters at Three Forks. Big, Holcomb, and Overflow creeks, which come together to form the West Fork are all good wild-trout streams above Three Forks. Of these, Holcomb Creek has the best access, since FS 86 parallels it for a distance above the junction. Holcomb Creek does receive some light stockings of hatchery trout along the road. Both Big and Holcomb creeks are only open for fishing during the regular state trout season.

Overflow Creek, which is a medium-sized stream, is open to year-round fishing. Road access to the creek is only possible in its headwaters via FS 868. When fishing Overflow above the FS 868 crossing, the state boundary is only a short distance upstream. Beyond that border, a North Carolina fishing license is required.

The Chattooga also forms the border between Georgia and South Carolina, and it is important to bear in mind that a valid South Carolina license is required to fish in any of the streams entering the river from the northeast side. It is legal to fish the main flow of the river from the South Carolina bank with a Georgia license, but not the feeder creeks.

Best access to the lower Chattooga, much of which simply cannot be reached by motorized vehicles, is just below Burrells Ford on FS 646 on the South Carolina side. This road crosses a bridge at the ford. Foot access is available downstream on the Bartram/Chattooga River trail system.

Fishing pressure tends to be fairly heavy around Burrells Ford, which is a favorite with campers. Moving downstream the angling activity falls off quickly, becoming only light on most of this section.

Upstream from Burrells Ford to the North Carolina border the Chattooga is one of the premier brown trout fisheries of Georgia. The stream is still big water, averaging 50 to 60 feet in width and is characterized by big, deep pools broken by shoals. No stocking is done on this section, which is primary trout water.

For a number of years this part of the river was managed as a wild brown trout fishery, and even today 95 percent of the fish taken will be browns. As one fishes further above Burrells Ford, fewer rainbow trout will be found. Brown trout of up to 10 pounds have been caught here, but these trout can be quite finicky when it comes to taking a lure, bait, or fly.

On one spring weekend of backpacking upstream from Burrells Ford, I managed to get in a few minutes of fly casting after we had made camp and before it got dark on Friday night. I was able to cast a dry fly on two runs before night fell, and on both I raised and landed brown trout longer than 11 inches. Oh yes, the fishing was going to be good and easy this weekend!

As you can guess, I was dead wrong. The next morning I flogged the water with everything in my fly box, while my fishing companions threw every imaginable lure and spinner at the fish. Our net result for the morning was one trout raised, which I failed to hook.

Adjourning back to camp, we had lunch. During the heat of the afternoon, when we figured the fishing would be slow (not that it could get any slower than what we had already endured), I agreed to give one of my campmates a lesson in fly casting.

We began the session on a shallow riffle area that was flowing beside our campsite. As soon as he mastered the skill of getting a few feet of fly line out onto the water, he began to raise trout. The fish were browns in the 8- to 10-inch range and they seemed to have abandoned all caution. I quickly had my own rod strung and was soon catching fish on the same flies that had drifted unmolested in the morning! Apparently something had triggered the trouts' feeding instincts during what had to be the least likely time of day for such activity.

Getting to these picky trout of the upper Chattooga is not too difficult, though it tends to be time consuming. Much of the riverbank above the ford is included in the federally mandated Ellicott Rock Wilderness Area. For that reason only foot travel is allowed.

The wilderness area takes its name from surveyor Andrew Ellicott who was commissioned in the early nineteenth century to lay out the state borders between Georgia, North Carolina, and South Carolina. Part of his legacy was a carving on a rock that lies on the riverbank. The stone is known as Ellicott Rock and marks the corner where the three states meet. It is important to trout anglers because it marks the upstream limit of the fishing range without a North Carolina license.

A sign stands in the middle of the streamside trail at the border, with an arrow pointing down to the water indicating the location of Ellicott Rock. The rock itself is not that evident, however. On my first trip upstream, I reached the sign and discovered two hikers sitting on the stream bank. After a cursory investigation of the surroundings, I could find no sign of the carving that was supposed to adorn one of the boulders at the location. When I asked the hikers if they had found it, they replied in the negative, going into great detail to describe the search they had just completed.

Having already been wading the river as I fished up to this point, I got back in the water and crossed to the other bank to look for the rock. After more fruitless searching, I waded back across. As I approached the boulder the two hikers were perched on, I saw the inscription dated 1813 carved just above the water line. Whether it is history or brown trout, the Chattooga River appears reluctant at times to yield its treasures to the visitor.

Fishing pressure is generally light to moderate on this upper part of the river, but foot access is not very strenuous on the Chattooga River trail that parallels the stream.

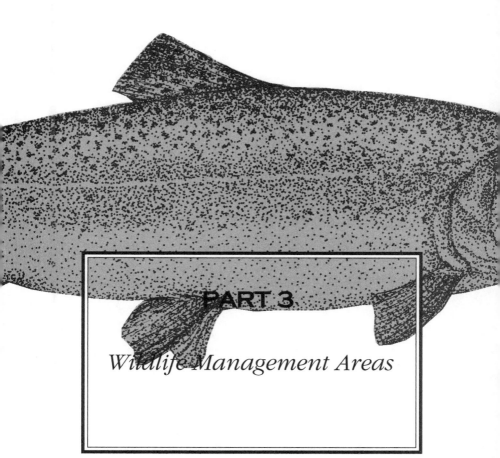

PART 3

Wildlife Management Areas

Georgia's Wildlife Management Area (WMA) system has been in existence since the 1930s and is designed to provide public lands for the enhancement and protection of wildlife resources. Along with this primary goal, these lands also offer a number of recreational opportunities such as hiking, camping, birdwatching, hunting, and fishing.

Although the Game and Fish Division of the Department of Natural Resources manages these WMAs, the state actually holds title to very little of this land in the northern third of the state. The bulk of it is owned by the US Forest Service and is leased to the state and open to public use. Other portions are held by private companies or individuals who have agreed to allow state biologists to manage the wildlife and fisheries on their land.

While these private landowners cooperate with the state to enhance and protect the resources, they are under no obligation to open their property to the public. For this reason, some lands included in WMAs are not open to general use and may even be posted. Rich Mountain and Coosawattee WMAs are examples of North Georgia tracts that contain large private holdings within their boundaries.

The streams on WMAs that are bordered by private land are governed by the same laws that were discussed earlier. The property owner has title to the midpoint of the stream, and if both shores are owned, the entire creek is on private property. Even if a creek is on a WMA, permission is required for fishing there unless the land is actually owned or leased by the state.

In discussing the smaller mountain trout streams of Georgia, I have established the arbitrary starting point of beginning with the streams that are farthest west and working to the east. It seems logical to look at the waters on each of the state's WMAs as a unit, beginning with Johns Mountain.

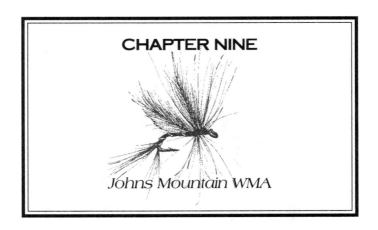

CHAPTER NINE

Johns Mountain WMA

Located in portions of Floyd, Gordon, Walker, and Whitfield counties in northwest Georgia, the Johns Mountain WMA has several features that set it apart from most of Georgia's other public trout fishing areas. To begin with, the 28,000 acres of US Forest Service and private timber company lands that make up the WMA are situated in the Armuchee Ranger District of the Chattahoochee National Forest. Separate from the bulk of the national forest found further east, this part of the Chattahoochee NF is west of an imaginary line from Dalton south to Calhoun and contains a mountainous spine of land composed of Dick Ridge, Horn Mountain, Johns Mountain, Mill Creek Mountain, and Rocky Face.

This southern extension of the Blue Ridge Mountains is just at the edge of the break line between Georgia's mountain region and the ridge-and-valley geophysical region that makes up most of the northwest corner of the state. As a result of this unique location, Johns Mountain WMA lies in an area of underground springs, porous limestone rock, and creeks that often dry up completely in the arid summer and fall months. All of these factors combine to make the area rather marginal trout fishing territory at best.

Johns Mountain WMA

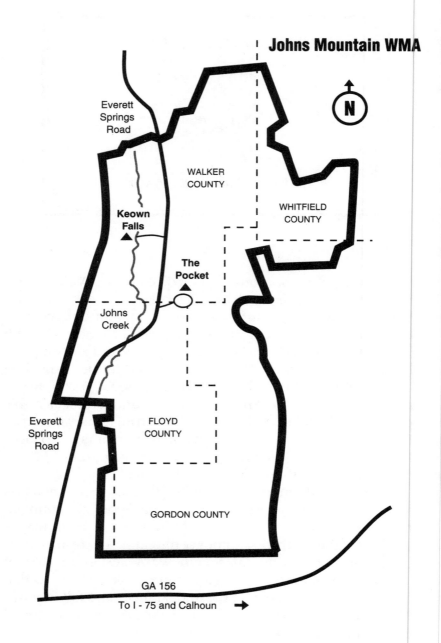

Everett Springs Road

WALKER COUNTY

WHITFIELD COUNTY

Keown Falls ▲

The Pocket ▲

Johns Creek

Everett Springs Road

FLOYD COUNTY

GORDON COUNTY

GA 156

To I - 75 and Calhoun ➡

N

JOHNS CREEK
SIZE: *Small*
ACCESS: *Easy*
SPECIES: *Stocked rainbow trout*

The only stream in the Johns Mountain WMA that is really worth mentioning as a trout-angling destination is Johns Creek. Rising in the northern part of the WMA on the slopes of Johns Mountain near Keown Falls, Johns Creek is fed by springs that bubble up from the bedrock at several locations along its course. The stream eventually empties into the Oostanaula River.

After just a cursory inspection of the facts, a trout angler is inclined to approach a fishing trip to Johns Mountain with a measure of excitement and anticipation. After all, here is a creek that originates in the cool, crystalline waters of limestone springs, then flows through a gentle valley. These waters teem with life in the form of crayfish, snails, and small minnows. All these features call to mind the world-renowned spring creeks that have made the fishing in central Pennsylvania and Montana legendary. Could it be that Georgia has such a stream of its own? Not quite.

Although it shares some common traits with those world-famous trout waters, Johns Creek falls short of its promise. Even though the springs issue forth with cold water and the stream stays cool even in the heat of August, it is only marginal as trout habitat. For one thing, the creek's slow, almost sluggish flow, is also inhabited by lowland, warm-water species of fish such as bass, bluegills, redbreasts, and an assortment of suckers, daces, and darters. These, of course, compete with the trout for food sources and living space.

Additionally, the trout have little cover in which to hide from predators, human or otherwise. Much of the stream is shallow and where deeper holes appear, the water is so clear that the trout are easily visible to anyone on the shore.

Needless to say, these fish get a lot of attention from visiting anglers.

Finally, the limestone rocks and silted pools must not offer much in the way of spawning habitat, since no small wild trout are evident even in the creek's riffle areas. Thus, Johns Creek is strictly a hatchery-supported, put-and-take fishery.

Catchable-sized rainbow trout are released into the public land sections of the stream throughout the season. As mentioned, these fish are easily spotted in the creek, so much of the action is sight-fishing. The vast majority of the angling pressure on Johns Creek is in the form of bait fishing from the bank. Casting spinners, small jigs, or even tiny crankbaits will also produce fish.

The bulk of the fish taken come from the larger, deeper pools on the creek. Though trout can be seen holding in some of the calmer shallow runs, they are very difficult to approach in this thin water and are easily spooked.

For the fly-fisher the sport is frustrating on Johns Creek. Despite the fact that conditions would seem to favor this type of angling and most of the creek is open enough to permit some long casts, getting favorable results is a rarity. As is usually true, the freshly-stocked hatchery trout do not adapt well to their new environment (most never live long enough to get a chance to adapt), and they seem oblivious to imitations of natural foods. It is extremely rare to get one of these fish to rise to the surface for a dry fly, and only occasionally do they show interest in wet flies or nymphs. These trout are much more inclined to ambush an unsuspecting kernel of corn or wad of cheese bait than an insect.

Johns Creek will usually have quite a few anglers along its banks during any weekend of the season. One piece of equipment that is practically never seen here is a pair of waders. That is because there are few situations that require getting in the water on Johns Creek.

Access is good from a paved county road that parallels the stream's fishable water in the public land section of the creek. Paths are worn along the shore between the spots where the road shoulder is at the water's edge. The surrounding foliage is open enough that an angler can find a vantage point from which to cast to any spot on the stream without wading.

To locate Johns Creek, take GA 156 west from its intersection with I-75 in Calhoun. The road makes several turns through intersections in Calhoun, but follow the signs for GA 156 at each of these. At 14.5 miles, turn right onto Everett Springs Road.

Johns Creek soon appears as you travel north on Everett Springs Road, but private farm land lies along both banks in this lower section. After crossing the creek a couple of times the road enters the WMA, and the public-use areas become obvious along the roadside. There are roughly 2.5 miles of fishable public water up to a point just north of the intersection with the road leading to Lake Marvin. This intersection is just south of The Pocket, which is a US Forest Service campground and picnic area on one of Johns Creek's feeder streams.

CHAPTER TEN

Cohutta WMA

For many anglers, a great deal of the allure of trout fishing lies in where it takes place. The remote, scenic mountain streams and rivers, which serve as home for the various branches of the trout family, provide the solitude, natural beauty, and wilderness mystique that completes this angling experience.

For those who want to challenge wild, stream-bred trout in such a pristine wilderness, the Cohutta WMA of northwest Georgia is a diamond in the rough just waiting to be discovered. Sprawling across 95,265 acres of rugged terrain in the Cohutta Mountains of Fannin, Gilmer, and Murray counties, this WMA contains many miles of quality trout streams ranging from tiny rivulets to full-fledged rivers. The pure, clear waters and remote location of these streams provide the perfect setting for some of the best trout fishing in Georgia. The creeks of the Cohuttas are home to healthy, naturally reproducing populations of rainbow and brown trout that will test the skill and patience of even the most experienced angler.

Georgia's second oldest WMA, the Cohutta has one of the more unusual histories of such preserves. First established in 1937 by workers of the Depression-era Civilian Conservation Corps, the WMA was far from being an instant success. The white-tailed deer that were reintroduced to the area multiplied and thrived, but the local human inhabitants of the region were not so accommodating to the idea of having a wildlife reserve in their backyard. Poaching was rampant, with dogs being used to chase the deer at all seasons and all times of the day and night. Fishing regulations were undoubtedly ignored as well during this period.

Conditions deteriorated to the point that the state withdrew the Cohutta Mountains from the WMA system in the early 1960s. The wildlife populations had been decimated, and the WMA was given up as a failure. Fortunately, within less than a decade local attitudes changed enough that wildlife managers gave the area another chance, and it was readmitted to the WMA system in 1969. Today the Cohutta WMA is the crown jewel of North Georgia natural areas.

A contributing factor to the Cohutta WMA's being Georgia's most primitive mountain reserve is the location of the Cohutta Wilderness Area within its boundaries. Comprised of roughly 37,000 acres surrounding the Conasauga and Jacks river valleys, it is the largest of the federally protected wilderness areas east of the Mississippi River. No motorized equipment has been allowed, and travel has been restricted to hiking or horseback riding only since the wilderness area was established by Congress in 1974.

To reach any of the streams in the Cohutta WMA requires at least several miles of driving on gravel Forest Service roads and, in many cases, an additional several miles of hiking on approach trails. The terrain, composed of lands owned by the Forest Service with a sprinkling of private enclaves, varies from 1,500 feet of elevation in the creek valleys to more than 4,000 feet at the peak of some mountains. Needless to say, this topography makes for some difficult travel. If, however, the thrill of a wilderness angling challenge is your goal, the effort will be well compensated in the Cohuttas.

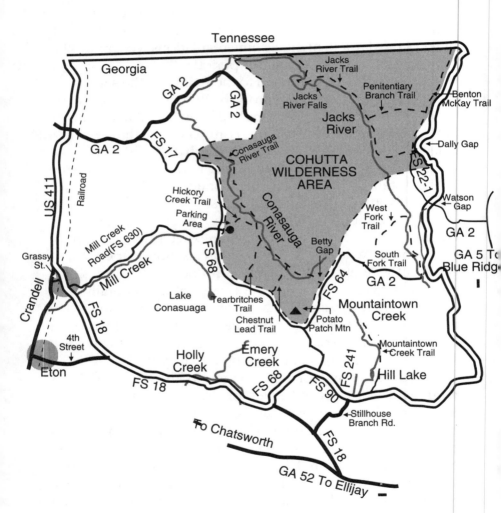

The best time of the year for fishing here is late April through early June when the spring rains have abated and streams are at normal levels. Not only will the fishing be at its peak, but the mountain scenery will be ablaze at different altitudes with the orange blossoms of wild azaleas and the pinks and whites of rhododendron and mountain laurel. Later on, with the coming of summer, the water levels begin to fall and the low, crystal-clear water makes the trout extremely wary and hard to approach. Even under normal conditions, of course, caution is a must to get close enough to have any chance of casting to the fish without spooking them.

An excellent map of the Cohutta Wilderness Area showing all the hiking trails can be ordered for a small fee from the Forest Service. The address to write is: US Forest Service, Distribution Center, Room 816, 1720 Peachtree Road NW, Atlanta, Georgia 30367.

JACKS RIVER
Size: *Large*
Access: *Difficult*
Species: *Wild brown and rainbow trout*

The Jacks River is the largest of the streams on the Cohutta WMA. The South Fork rises in Sassafras Gap on the southern edge of the WMA and flows northward to join the West Fork in the shadows of Dyer Mountain. Both forks are extremely small, bushy streams, but they do harbor rainbows in the 7- to 10-inch range, and the South Fork will sometimes yield a brown of 12 inches or better. To the north, the Jacks flows a distance through private lands before emerging in the Cohutta Wilderness Area, just above the river's junction with Bear Branch. For the next 15 miles the Jacks descends through a narrow valley surrounded by stately hemlocks, finally emptying into the Conasauga River near the Tennessee border. Besides providing plenty of action for 9- to 12-inch rainbows, the Jacks will also produce some trophy fish, with browns of up to 9 pounds having been caught.

There is road access to the Jacks in its headwaters, but the rest of the river in the wilderness area must be approached over rugged trails that are steeply graded. The Jacks River Trail begins in Dally Gap and parallels Bear Branch for two miles in a westerly direction before striking the river. It then turns north to follow the river its entire length through the Wilderness Area. For most of the way the trail follows the old roadbed of a turn-of-the-century narrow-gauge railway that was used by loggers to haul out the first-growth American chestnut trees that covered the mountains before being wiped out by the blight in the 1930s. In places, the old cross ties are still visible protruding from the pathway.

The Wilderness Area section of the river is also accessible by Penitentiary Branch Trail, which approaches the river from the east to intersect the Jacks River Trail. Six miles long, it shares the path with the Benton McKay Trail for 3 miles as they climb out of Dally Gap. Penitentiary Branch Trail then splits off to follow a steep, abandoned logging road to the river.

Camping is allowed all along the river in the Wilderness Area, but it is suggested that sites be limited to those previously used to minimize damage to the natural features of the area. One particularly popular camping area is around the Jacks River Falls near the midpoint of the river's passage through the Wilderness Area. The stream tumbles over a 10-foot ledge into a natural swimming pool, then cascades down a 50-foot drop to form one of the most scenic and powerful falls in the Georgia mountains.

If you plan to hike for any distance on the Jacks River Trail, be prepared to get your feet wet. The trail crosses the river forty-four times.

To get to the Jacks River, take GA 5 north from Blue Ridge for 3.5 miles. Turn left on Old GA 2 and continue until it becomes a gravel road. Proceed to its intersection with

Forest Service Road 22-1 at Watson Gap. To reach the headwaters, go left, staying on GA 2 for 3.5 miles to the bridge over the South Fork. The South Fork Trail parallels the river up to its junction with the West Fork.

For the Wilderness Area section of the river, take a sharp right turn at Watson Gap onto FS 22-1 and go 3 miles to Dally Gap and the Jacks River and Penitentiary Branch trailheads.

CONASAUGA RIVER
Size: *Medium to small*
Access: *Difficult*
Species: *Wild brown and rainbow trout*

The valley of the Conasauga River is one of the most pristine areas of the Georgia mountains. Surrounded by peaks that rise up to 4,000 feet of elevation, the valley has remained unaffected by civilization. From its headwaters near Betty Gap in the Wilderness Area, the Conasauga flows northward and parallel to the Jacks until they join in the Alaculsy Valley.

Although smaller than the Jacks, the Conasauga rivals it in numbers of trout. But, in spite of the numbers of fish present, the Conasauga is not easy fishing. Because there is no development along its course, its waters are incredibly pure and crystal clear. Conasauga River trout are extremely wary and will test the stalking and approach skills of even a master angler.

The predominant species in the Conasauga is the rainbow, but browns are also present. Especially in the late summer and fall, browns of 12 to 16 inches will occasionally fall victim to large spinners or streamers.

As on the Jacks, all camping is the primitive backpack variety, and access to the river by trail is at least as difficult as in the Jacks' valley.

The headwaters of the Conasauga can be approached on the Conasauga River Trail that begins in Betty Gap. This trail is 2 miles long, and the first quarter mile or so drops steeply before leveling out to a gentle slope for the remainder of its descent. The trail then follows the river north for most of its course through the Wilderness Area.

Two additional trails approach the river in its middle section, with Chestnut Lead Trail descending along Chestnut Creek for 2 miles to the river. Just to the north, 4-mile long Tearbritches Trail also enters the river valley from the west. Both descend steeply, with either being a good entry point to the stream. However, avoid hiking out on Tearbritches. Whoever laid out the trail apparently had never heard of switchbacks. The path goes straight uphill, and you will feel like you have been dragging your nose on the ground by the time you reach the trailhead. It is one of the most strenuous trails in the north Georgia mountains and should be used only as an entry point.

To reach the lower section of the river, Hickory Creek Trail can be used. It is a 3-mile walk on an old logging road, some of which parallels Little Rough Creek, and is the easiest access point to the Conasauga.

To find the Conasauga River, go 6.9 miles north from the town square in Chatsworth on US 411. Turn right on Grassy Street. There is a street sign at the intersection. Continue on this road until it crosses the railroad tracks and ends in an intersection. Turn to the right and then back to the left on FS 630 at the Crandall Post Office. After 7 miles the road crosses West Cowpens Road. Go straight through the intersection, continuing for a half mile to the parking area for the Hickory Creek Trail.

To reach the other approach trails, take a right at the intersection onto West Cowpens Road (FS 17). At the turnoff for Lake Conasauga, this road will change to FS 68. Parking areas for Tearbritches and Chestnut Lead trails are on the left of the road. Continue straight at the intersection on top of Potato Patch Mountain, following FS 64 for about 2 miles to reach the trailhead for the Conasauga River Trail at Betty Gap.

MOUNTAINTOWN CREEK

SIZE: *Small*
ACCESS: *Difficult*
SPECIES: *Wild brown and rainbow trout*
SPECIAL REGULATIONS: *Artificial lures only*

Mountaintown Creek flows south from Betty Gap, exiting the WMA and eventually emptying into the Coosawattee River. It is the only stream in the Cohutta WMA that has special regulations, with the portion above the dam at Hill Lake restricted to artificial lures only. The dam—designated as Soil Conservation Structure #2 in the Department of Natural Resources' trout guide—lies about a mile upstream from the southern edge of the management area.

The stretch from the lake downstream is open under regular trout regulations and has a primitive campground at streamside. Fire rings, a footbridge across the creek, and portable toilets are located at the site. This part of the stream flows through both private and public lands and is hard to fish because of rocky wading conditions and heavily foliaged banks. There are a number of deeper pools along this section, however, that often yield brown trout of 10 to 12 inches.

Due to the problem of identifying the private property, it is best to fish only the portion of the creek below the lake that is in the immediate vicinity of the campground. Encountering cabins on the bank is a good indicator that the edge of the public land has been reached. All the land above Hill Lake is on public property.

Above Hill Lake, Mountaintown is a bit more open, making both spin and fly casting possible. Up until the summer of 1990, this part of the stream ran through long stretches where it broadened and became so shallow that few areas of holding water could be found. The Game and Fish Division, aided by volunteers supplied by local Trout Unlimited chapters, installed in-stream structures that summer to redirect the current and provide more pockets suitable for trout habitat. The fishing in this stretch of water picked up almost immediately upon completion of the work.

A good population of wild rainbows are present, with fish up to 12 inches not uncommon. Some brown trout also make their home in the stream. Most of the fish encountered will run only 7 to 9 inches long and are generally very wary. This part of Mountaintown is less enjoyable for the novice and more suited to the experienced angler who likes a tactical challenge.

To reach Mountaintown Creek, travel west from Ellijay for approximately 19 miles on US 52 and turn right onto Conasauga Creek Road (FS 18). Follow this paved road, which soon changes to gravel, for 1.5 miles and take a right on Stillhouse Branch Road. After another 2 miles you reach the junction with FS 90. Stay to the right at this intersection and go 3/4 of a mile to the bridge over Mountaintown Creek. The dirt road (FS 241) on the left just before the bridge will take you to the primitive campground. The road fords Bear Creek, which is easily passable for most passenger cars.

Past the bridge a couple of hundred yards is another dirt road on the left marked with a small sign for Hill Lake. It is 1.75 miles on this road to the lake, but the going is very rough and best traveled in four-wheel-drive vehicles. Above Hill Lake, Mountaintown Creek Trail follows an old logging road to provide foot access to the headwaters of the stream.

HOLLY CREEK

> SIZE: *Medium to small*
> ACCESS: *Easy to moderate*
> SPECIES: *Stocked brook trout, wild and stocked brown and rainbow trout*

Holly Creek is located on the southern edge of the WMA, to the west of Mountaintown Creek, and is a tributary of the Conasauga River. It is the only stream in the Cohutta WMA that receives regular stockings of trout. Catchable-sized rainbows and brook trout are released in the lower sections of the stream where there is good road access. This part of the creek is ideal for family groups to fish, as it consists of large pools alongside FS 18.

Farther up, where the stream is away from the road, there is good fishing for wild rainbows in both Holly Creek and its major tributary, Emery Creek. Emery Creek enters the main stream from the left about a mile above the road. A hiking trail along the creek provides good access up to where the creeks join.

Above the intersection with Emery Creek, Holly Creek runs though a small, steep valley that is fairly strenuous to travel. This terrain eliminates much of the fishing pressure one would expect to find associated with such a stream. As a result, the creek can provide some interesting and uncrowded angling to the person willing to put out the effort to get to it.

To reach Holly Creek, go north on US 411 from the square in Chatsworth for 3.8 miles to the only traffic light in the town of Eton. Turn right onto a street that is designated 4th Avenue, though there is no street sign at this intersection. After the right turn from US 411, stay on this road until it turns to gravel. At 6.5 miles from US 411, Holly Creek will appear on the left.

MILL CREEK
Size: *Small*
Access: *Easy to moderate*
Species: *Stocked rainbows*

The final stream to be mentioned on the Cohutta WMA is Mill Creek. It flows west to exit the management area near the village of Crandall and eventually empties into the Conasauga River.

Despite its small size, Mill Creek is surprisingly open, and there is room here to use any type of fishing equipment. In the summer and fall, especially, when the water is low, the stream is crystal clear and rather slow moving.

Viewed from the gravel road that runs along the stream, Mill Creek looks like good trout water. Unfortunately, its appearance is deceptive. At best the creek is marginal trout habitat. Most of its fish life consists of redeye bass, bream, suckers, darters, dace, and chubs. Some occasional plantings of trout take place, and a few of these stocked fish can be spotted in the pools throughout the season.

Although the creek is almost constantly in sight of FS 630, it is also in a ravine well below the level of the road along most of its course. For that reason, and its marginal trout habitat, fishing pressure is generally light along most of its length.

Some good access is afforded at primitive camping areas on the lower portions of the creek and also at a couple of hunting camps farther up the stream. All of these are easily found along the Forest Service road.

Directions for Mill Creek are the same as those for the Conasauga River. Hard to miss, the creek is often visible from FS 630 on the right of the roadway as it climbs the mountains.

CHAPTER ELEVEN

Rich Mountain WMA

The Rich Mountain Wildlife Management Area near Ellijay in the northwest quadrant of the state is one of those enigmas of Georgia trout angling that makes the sport so frustrating. On a map the WMA looks quite extensive. It contains a National Wilderness Area as well as several fishable trout streams. It would seem to be a perfect place to spend a few days exploring new creeks and tangling with some trout.

Well, so much for impressions gleaned from maps. Although the Rich Mountain WMA contains 22,061 acres of land, probably half of that acreage is privately held. Most of these private acres are also posted, leaving only the Forest Service holdings open to the public. Included in the public lands are 9,649 acres of the Rich Mountain Wilderness Area.

The situation on the trout streams of the area is even more misleading than is the land area. Such streams as Big, Rock, Stanley, and Turniptown creeks are found on the Rich Mountain WMA, but, in fact, only about half of Stanley Creek is on open public land, and virtually none of the fishable water of the others is accessible to the visiting angler.

In the case of Turniptown Creek, which is a favorite of former President Jimmy Carter, a large portion of the stream is

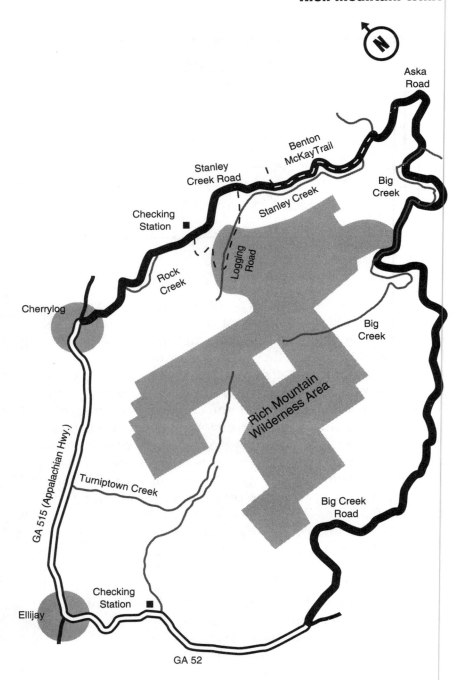

within the Walnut Mountain Resort where Mr. Carter has a cabin. Big and Rock creeks both skirt along the borders of the area, but with the exception of a couple of hundred scattered yards on each, they are on private, posted lands. The lower portion of Stanley Creek highlights the problem on this WMA. The sign that identifies it as an artificial-lure-only stream sits in the front yard of a private residence on Stanley Creek Road. But from this point on the stream, it is still about 3 or 4 miles to the first water that is open to public fishing on the creek.

Because of this confused situation, the only stream on the Rich Mountain WMA to be covered in this guide is the upper half of Stanley Creek.

STANLEY CREEK

SIZE: *Small*
ACCESS: *Moderate*
SPECIES: *Wild rainbow trout*
SPECIAL REGULATIONS: *Artificial lures only*

Stanley Creek is one of those jewels that I almost hate to mention. For a combination of reasons it is very lightly fished, in spite of deserving more attention than it gets. Unfortunately, it is such a small resource that it will not take much to overcrowd it. Now, having mentioned the downside, let me add a few words of encouragement.

In the past, Stanley Creek has rarely been stocked, but supports a reproducing population of wild rainbows. As mentioned earlier, it is also restricted to the use of artificial lures on the WMA. Additionally, reaching most of the public water requires a mile or two of walking. These factors eliminate many potential anglers, who, in general, are reluctant to fish a stream unless they are assured that the state's stocking trucks pay regular visits to the water. Many of these anglers also prefer to use bait rather than feathers or metal, and they display a distinct distaste for having to walk out of sight of their cars in order to fish.

In light of those facts, I am less hesitant to talk about Stanley Creek. Probably 80 percent of the state's trout anglers would not put out the effort to fish it even if they knew about the stream. Few anglers are likely to stumble onto it by accident, either, because of the buffer zone of private land that makes finding the public water via automobile difficult. Also, once found, the stream's appearance can be deceptive.

On my initial visit to the creek, I fished for about a quarter of a mile upstream from the first public land access. At that point the creek ran through a stretch of narrow and shallow water with heavily overgrown banks and an extremely tight canopy of foliage. Fishing was virtually impossible on this stretch of stream, which offered little encouragement in the form of promising-looking holding water. Turning back toward my car, I wrote Stanley Creek off as worthy of only a few quick casts if I happened to be in the area again in the future.

It was several years later, during a winter squirrel hunt on the WMA, that I discovered that the creek on the other side of the thicket offered another mile or more of fishable water on up into the Wilderness Area. I suspect that more than a few other anglers have made the same incorrect assumptions I did about the stream.

For those hardy souls who do persevere, the area open to the public begins at a wildlife clearing where the main branch of Stanley is joined by Falls Branch. To find this stream intersection, take the Appalachian Highway (GA 515) north from Ellijay toward Blue Ridge. Exit onto old GA 5 at Cherrylog. Take Stanley Creek Road east (the paved road running past Rock Creek Baptist Church and parallel to Rock Creek). The road changes to dirt after a few miles. Stay on it until you pass the WMA checking station. A little farther the road crests the Tennessee Valley Divide at Stanley Gap and starts downhill. The streams off the southwest side of the mountains from which you approached flow into the Coosa/Alabama river system, and those ahead of you flow northeast to feed the

Toccoa River in the Tennessee/Mississippi river system.

After crossing Stanley Gap, watch for a small wooden bridge and, on the left, a cleared area where hikers and anglers park their cars. This is where the Benton McKay Trail crosses the road, and the blazes for the trail are evident along Falls Branch to the left of the road. To the right, walking across a wildlife clearing will put you on Stanley Creek.

All of the trout I have taken from the main stem of Stanley Creek have been wild, stream-bred rainbows. These fish will run up to 10 inches, and there are some pools that have the potential for larger fish. Rumors of large trout coming from Stanley Creek persist among local anglers, but an $11^{1}/_{2}$–inch rainbow is the biggest I have personally seen caught and released.

Undoubtedly, there are also brown trout present in the stream system, but they are not common, and I have yet to hook one on this creek. At least some of the small brooklets that feed Stanley Creek also contain native brook trout. As is always the case, these hardy survivors will be found in the extreme headwaters above a natural barrier such as a waterfall.

Like the other managed streams in the state that restrict the type of tackle allowed and receive no hatchery fish, Stanley offers a higher caliber of angling than most creeks its size. This angling, however, can be quite tight. Short spinning rods matched to ultralight reels can be used, while a fly-fisher experienced on mountain streams can also find room to cast, although it will not be easy.

Upstream from the wildlife clearing, an old logging road descends from Stanley Creek Road and fords the creek at a shallow rocky crossing. This spot was the area of my original discouragement. By following the logging road up the left side of the creek for a short way, you can bypass some hard-to-fish and rather unproductive water. The path soon rejoins the creek; and a series of drops and potholes will be evident. These continue upstream into the Rich Mountain Wilderness Area.

It is also possible to reach this part of the stream by coming over the mountain on foot from the WMA checking station. Across from the checking station a gravel road joins Stanley Creek Road. A few hundred feet up this side road will be a fork, the left branch of which is in very poor shape. This is the other end of the logging road that eventually parallels Stanley Creek. Getting to the creek from here, however, requires climbing over the mountain ridge. At the crest of the ridge where another dirt track crosses the logging road, a sign (in poor repair as of this writing) identifies the Rich Mountain Wilderness Area. Continuing down the other slope of the ridge soon puts you on Stanley Creek where it exits the Wilderness Area.

This approach to the creek is one best reserved for anglers who are in shape and love an adventure. It is much easier to get on the water from the Falls Branch side of the gap.

Regardless of the direction of your approach to the stream, the pool at the Wilderness Area boundary generally holds a decent trout or two. Be aware that careless blundering onto the creek from either direction is guaranteed to spook the fish and send them scurrying for cover.

CHAPTER TWELVE

Dawson Forest WMA

The Dawson Forest WMA is located entirely in Dawson County in the north-central portion of the state and is the most southerly of the wildlife management areas that contains trout water. More than its location, however, makes Dawson Forest unique among the state preserves. This WMA has an unusual history.

The main portion of the preserve is made up of an almost square, 10,000-acre tract of land that once belonged to Lockheed Corporation and was the site of a US Air Force experimental nuclear reactor during the 1950s. When abandoned by the Air Force and Lockheed, the land was purchased by the City of Atlanta as a possible site for an airport to serve the city. The tract is still owned by Atlanta, but now seems unlikely ever to be developed as an air field.

The other portion of the Dawson Forest WMA is composed of a narrow corridor of about 5,000 acres of land owned by the Game and Fish Division of the Georgia Department of Natural Resources. The Amicalola River flows south through this valley and eventually empties into the Etowah River in the western portion of the WMA's Atlanta lands.

At one point during the early eighties the entire Amicalola valley was under consideration by the National Park Service

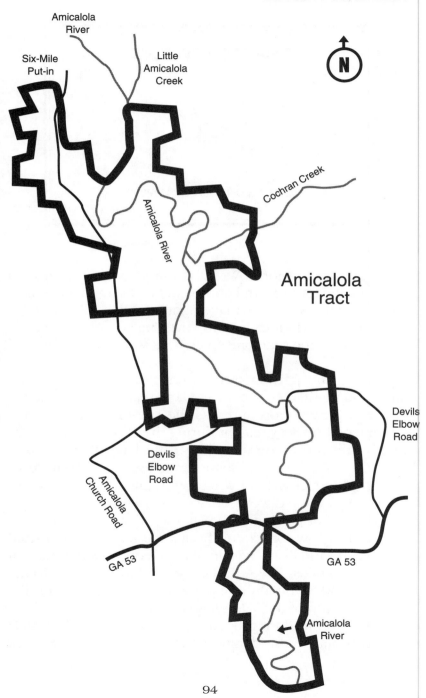

for inclusion in what would have been America's first National River Park. The idea was to create a park that stretched from the headwaters of a river to its mouth. The Amicalola was one of three rivers nationwide that made it to the final list for consideration.

The criteria used to evaluate the rivers were whether they had shorelines that were virtually undeveloped and had a minimum of road crossings. In the case of the Amicalola, it is very close to being in a natural state and is crossed by only two highways and two Forest Service roads.

The plan for such a park was eventually put on a back burner by the Park Service, and the Amicalola was dropped from consideration altogether. Because a major portion of the watershed was already owned by state and local governments, the resource was considered to be in safe hands.

Although the WMA contains major portions of both the Amicalola and Etowah rivers, the only stretch of interest to the trout angler is the portion of the Amicalola upstream from the GA 53 bridge. The other waters might hold some trout but are basically warm-water flows more suited to other species.

AMICALOLA RIVER
Size: *Large*
Access: *Easy*
Species: *Stocked brown and rainbow trout*
Special Regulations: *Open year-round from Devils Elbow to GA 53*

On many maps this stream is identified as a creek rather than a river, but by North Georgia standards it definitely has the volume to qualify as the latter. Its headwaters on Little Amicalola Creek are on the southern slopes of Frosty Mountain, north of Amicalola Falls State Park. After plunging over the 600-foot high cascade that gives the park its name, the stream joins with other small feeders to form the river, which then flows down to the Etowah. Below the state park the river is on private land, so it is only the portion from GA 53 to just above Six-Mile Put-in that is accessible to visiting anglers.

The Amicalola's main reputation is as a white-water canoe stream. In fact, its name is derived from the Cherokee Indian word for "tumbling water." In all there are roughly 9.5 miles of fishable trout waters on the river from Six-Mile down to the GA 53 bridge. As mentioned, trout will show up in the river below this bridge, but they are not common.

Throughout its flow the river is only a marginal trout stream that requires regular stockings to support the fishery. Rainbow and brown trout in the 8- to 10-inch range are stocked, and very little carryover of fish seems to occur from year to year.

The Amicalola has plenty of room on the stream for bait, spin, or fly fishing. The major drawback to angling is that there are only three access points. Besides Six-Mile and the GA 53 bridge, the only other point is at Devils Elbow where a gravel road intersects the river. A covered bridge dating from 1897 existed at this point until 1977, when vandals put a torch to it, and a modern span now crosses the stream.

The most practical method of covering the waters of the Amicalola is by float-fishing. The stream will accommodate canoes, float-rings, or johnboats. Some local anglers even fish it while drifting in regular automobile inner tubes.

There are several tricky rapids in this part of the river, so caution is necessary during a float. A sign, which includes a map of the river, is on the roadside at the approach to Six-Mile Put-in and should be studied before venturing downstream. Below GA 53, the Amicalola becomes a serious white-water stream, rated by many as second only to the state's fabled Chattooga River. These raging waters, which hold very few trout, are best left by the angler to the canoe enthusiasts.

In order to reach the Amicalola, travel north on GA 400 from Atlanta to the intersection with GA 53 and turn left. Stay on GA 53 through Dawsonville, until you cross the Amicalola and proceed another 1.5 miles to Amicalola Church Road.

Turn right and follow this road to its intersection with Devils Elbow Road.

Another right turn onto Devils Elbow Road leads to the river in about a mile. Parking areas are visible at several spots along the stream near the bridge. There is usually ample room to handle the vehicles of both anglers and canoeists at this point.

To reach Six-Mile Put-in, continue north on Amicalola Church Road another mile until it changes to gravel. At 3.5 miles you reach a fork in the road. Stay to the right for an additional third of a mile. The sign for Six-Mile Put-in will be at the intersection with a gravel track running off to the right of the road. This track leads to the river and a primitive camping area on the shore of the stream.

CHAPTER THIRTEEN

Blue Ridge WMA

The Blue Ridge WMA is the oldest in Georgia's wildlife management area system. It was established when Civilian Conservation Corps work crews entered the area to mark it off in 1937. As a result, it has been spared many of the ravages of development suffered by other areas during the last 50 years.

Lying in an area that has always enjoyed a colorful history, the WMA is located about a dozen miles west of the historic gold-mining town of Dahlonega, where America's first gold rush occurred during the 1820s and '30s. The first overseer of Blue Ridge was Ranger Arthur Woody, a veritable legend in the vicinity who almost single-handedly was responsible for the reintroduction and establishment of white-tailed deer in the Georgia mountains during the 1940s.

Composed of 38,900 acres in Fannin, Lumpkin, and Union counties, virtually the entire area is made up of land owned by the US Forest Service. Blue Ridge WMA covers some fairly rough and mountainous terrain, but, for the most part, still provides good access to all of its fishable trout streams.

The creeks in the area that flow off the north slope of the mountains are the headwaters of the Toccoa River, while those across the ridge flowing south eventually enter the

Etowah River. Through the center portion of the WMA, the Appalachian Trail winds along the crest of this ridge that divides the watersheds and is often used unofficially to divide the WMA into the upper and lower Blue Ridge. In talking about the streams. The upper area will be covered first, then the lower Blue Ridge.

NOONTOOTLA CREEK
SIZE: *Medium*
ACCESS: *Easy*
SPECIES: *Wild brown and rainbow trout*
SPECIAL REGULATIONS: *Artificial lures only, restricted creel limit*

A few stray beams of early spring sun slipped through the canopy of hemlock and poplar to break the shaded surface of the moving water as it slid into the deeper pool below. The No. 14 slate-green caddis imitation resisted the downward tug of the swirls in the current and bobbed downstream, bouyed by its hackles and woodchuck wings.

As the fly swept past a drooping rhododendron limb that touched the water, a dark shape rose from the run to suck the caddis from the surface only an instant before the current would have engulfed it. When the fish felt the bite of the hook, it first turned downstream, leaped clear of the water and landed, then turned across the current to add the weight of the moving waters to its own efforts to pull free.

I grudgingly gave the trout some line as I moved cautiously downstream with it, trying to keep the fine tippet tight, while not taxing it to the breaking point. In spite of my efforts, I was forced to let the fish slip into the next pool downstream. As I tried to follow, my feet slid across a flat, submerged rock, and I took a seat, with the icy flow of the creek swallowing me to mid-chest.

Fortunately, I managed to keep a tight line, and the fish was still on when I finally struggled back to my feet. The battle

Blue Ridge WMA

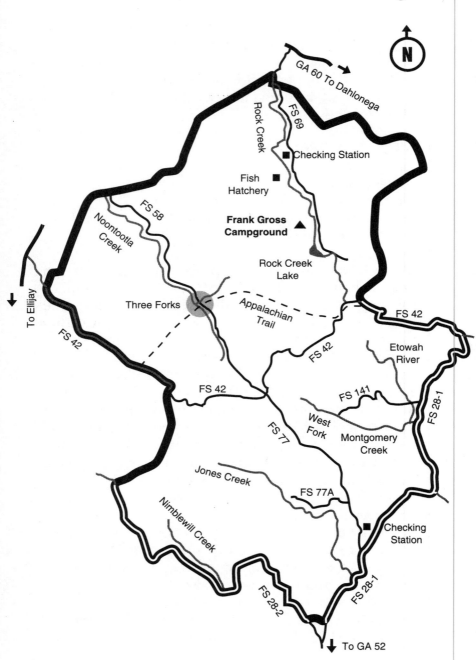

soon ended in a shallow eddy of that lower pool when I slipped the landing net under a thick-bodied, richly-colored, wild rainbow trout of 13 inches.

This rainbow was a respectable fish regardless of where it was caught, and knowing that it had come from a small Southern Appalachian stream added to the moment. The fact that I had fooled such a fish in that environment made the trout a veritable trophy. As the gently revived and released rainbow swam back into the current, the best part of the sensation was knowing that the stream held even better fish.

It is just such episodes as the preceding one from a recent mid-summer visit that make Noontootla Creek the premier stream of the Blue Ridge WMA. On most small Southern trout streams, a fish of 13 to 14 inches would be the catch of the season, but on Noontootla, it would more likely only earn bragging rights for the day.

The creek contains both wild brown and rainbow trout, having received no stockings since the mid-1960s. Rainbows and browns in the 14- to 16-inch and larger bracket are a possibility, and trout of 11 to 13 inches are common. While the average size of a wild trout on most Georgia streams will run 6 to 8 inches, on Noontootla the average is closer to 9 and 10 inches.

This above-average fishing is produced by a set of regulations that, in effect, make Noontootla a catch-and-release fishery. Only artificial lures may be used, and the creel limit is one fish per day that must be 16 inches or larger. These regulations apply to Noontootla and to all of its tributaries on the Blue Ridge WMA.

Part of the reason that Noontootla was chosen for management as a special-regulation stream lies in the pro-tected nature of its watershed. From its headwaters near Winding Stair Gap to the point where it empties into the Toccoa River, the bulk of its course is on the WMA and National Forest land.

Although early stockings of rainbow and brown trout led to the disappearance of the native brook trout, except in the headwaters of some feeder streams, Noontootla proved to be ideal for its new inhabitants. Self-sustaining breeding populations of both the browns and rainbows are now found in the creek.

The imposition of special regulations has had a marked effect on the stream in that angling pressure has been fairly low since their introduction in the mid-1960s. In fact, the average number of anglers on Noontootla fell from more than 60 per day before the regulations to fewer than 10 per day for the next decade. Although the total number has grown in recent years, the average number of anglers per day has not increased because the stream is now open to fishing every day during the season, instead of the weekend-only limitations of those earlier years. Especially during the week, it is possible to fish the stream in virtual solitude.

This lack of pressure is particularly surprising because a gravel Forest Service road parallels the entire length of the creek providing excellent access. Undoubtedly, the preoccupation of many local trout anglers with putting some fish in the frying pan plays a large part in the low pressure, as evidenced by surveys that have shown more than 50 percent of those fishing the stream come from metropolitan Atlanta, some 60 miles to the south. Local residents of Fannin County, in which the creek is located, comprise only 40 percent of the anglers.

Another statistic from these surveys on Noontootla that is uncharacteristic of most Southern Appalachian streams shows that more than 40 percent of the anglers on the creek are fly-fishers. On other Georgia artificial-only streams it is often possible to fish an entire day and meet only anglers using spinning gear.

Although virtually all the keeper-sized fish reported each year are browns, stream surveys by state biologists have found that rainbows of 10 to 14 inches are common in Noontootla. These studies have also found that browns of 12 inches or longer make up 20 percent of the population of that species in the creek. While probably not impressive by Chattahoochee or Toccoa River tailrace standards, these statistics point to some above-average fishing, particularly for wild, stream-bred fish.

Throughout its course on the Blue Ridge WMA, Noontootla would be considered a small to medium-sized stream. In its headwaters above Three Forks (where the Appalachian Trail crosses the stream) and on all its tributaries, the fishing is tight. There is room, however, on the main stem of the creek to allow for fly-fishing.

The only sizeable feeder stream on the WMA is Long Creek, which enters Noontootla at Three Forks. Some instream structures have been added recently by Forest Service workers and Trout Unlimited volunteers in its lower stretches below Long Creek Falls. The falls lie roughly a mile upstream from the junction of the creeks. The Appalachian and Benton McKay trails travel on the same footpath through here, following Long Creek and providing access to its upstream portions.

Of course, the major attraction of the Noontootla Creek watershed is the possibility of coming face-to-snout with a true trophy trout in a small stream. These meetings, however, can prove very frustrating as well as exciting.

That was very much the case several years back when I faced off with a large brown in Long Creek. At the end of October several companions and I were winding up a three-day hike along the Appalachian Trail. We had planned to reach Three Forks in time to allow for some fishing on the final day of the season.

Soon after shedding our backpacks beside Long Creek, just upstream of its mouth at Noontootla, I discovered a brownie in a shallow pool. Easily 20 inches or better, this old-timer had apparently answered the urge to move upstream into Long Creek for the fall spawn. As I watched, the fish would come from beneath an undercut bank and swim leisurely up the pool. It would then reverse course, move to the foot of the run, and scatter the minnows in the shallows before returning to its lair under the bank.

After watching several of these matinee performances, I unlimbered my fly rod and tossed a streamer across to the opposite shore while the trout was under the bank. After the fish reappeared and made its upstream swing, I stripped the fly across the current in front of its nose as the trout headed back toward the shallows. This veteran, who had undoubtedly endured many such encounters, took a perfunctory look at the fly and continued about its business. During the rest of the afternoon the old brown proceeded to ignore every fly and spinning lure that our group displayed. Although we managed not to spook our prey, we also failed to catch its interest.

I did return to the pool on opening day of the season the next April just on the off chance that the big brown trout was actually a permanent resident of Long Creek. I was surprised, upon crossing over to the north side of Winding Stair Gap, to find the slopes down to Long Creek still covered with several inches of snow. I was much less surprised to find the shallow pool empty. The brown had long since dropped back down the creek to the larger waters of Noontootla.

As mentioned earlier, access to Noontootla Creek is quite good via Forest Service Road 58. To reach it from the north, take Big Creek Road from GA 52 just east of Ellijay, and turn right onto FS 58. Approaching the creek from the south over Winding Stair Road (FS 77) can be a chancy affair. This steep, gravel road is sometimes closed and impassable because of adverse weather conditions.

ROCK CREEK

SIZE: *Small to medium*
ACCESS: *Easy*
SPECIES: *Stocked brook and brown trout,
stocked and wild rainbow trout*

Rock Creek is the other major stream flowing north from the Blue Ridge WMA to join the Toccoa River. Its fishery, however, bears little resemblance to that of Noontootla Creek, which it parallels. Rock Creek provides the upper Blue Ridge area with a put-and-take fishery that is tame enough for the whole family.

A medium-sized stream in its lower reaches, Rock Creek is heavily stocked with keeper-sized trout, many of which come from the federal trout hatchery located at the junction of the main creek with its feeder stream, Mill Creek. Also located on the creek is Rock Creek Lake, which provides a still-water option for trout fishing. The lake covers several acres and is open under general trout regulations. Above the lake, Rock Creek qualifies as only a small stream, but this part of the creek is also stocked.

As mentioned earlier, the state record brown trout was taken from Rock Creek back in 1967, but the 18-plus-pound fish was an escaped brood fish from the hatchery. Most trout here will be 8- to 12-inch, freshly planted fish, although an occasional wild rainbow will also turn up. As with most stocked streams, rainbow trout will be the species most often encountered.

For those who like trout fishing to be a community affair, Rock Creek is perfect. It gets extensive use from family groups, and the Forest Service operates the Frank Gross campground, which is located streamside between the lake and the fish hatchery. Below the hatchery, the stream has many primitive campsites along its course. Expect the angling pressure to be moderate to heavy on Rock Creek at all times of the season.

Access is excellent. FS 69 parallels the creek throughout the WMA, from above Rock Creek Lake to the intersection with GA 60, located northwest of Dahlonega. After passing Deep Hole Forest Service Campground on GA 60, watch for the gravel FS 69 on the left.

NIMBLEWILL CREEK
Size: *Small*
Access: *Easy*
Species: *Stocked brown trout and stocked and wild rainbow trout*

Turning next to the streams of the lower Blue Ridge WMA, we begin with Nimblewill Creek. This small creek is the most southerly of the streams on the WMA. Rising on the slopes of Frosty Mountain, between Amicalola Falls State Park and Springer Mountain, it flows to the southeast and eventually becomes part of the Etowah River.

Nimblewill is heavily stocked with keeper trout throughout the season and is the most frequently fished of the streams on the lower Blue Ridge reservation, primarily, of course, by bait anglers. Most of the planted fish are rainbows in the 8- to 10-inch class, although some native fish of the same species do live in the stream as well. With a Forest Service road paralleling much of the stream, and campsites liberally disbursed along the creek, Nimblewill is very crowded on opening day, as well as holidays and many weekends.

One assumption that is often made by anglers is that freshly released hatchery trout are easy marks for the first angler to visit the pool they have been dumped in. In many cases this proves to be true, but not always.

While fishing on Nimblewill on one occasion, I came upon a pool about 8 to 10 feet wide, maybe 20 feet long, and no more than 3 feet deep at any point. From the streamside litter, it was obvious that the pool had been heavily fished during the day. In spite of this fishing pressure, a pod of about a dozen stockers of up to 12 inches could be seen holding in some slick water just off the main current. I added my artificial offerings to the array of baits with which they had been accosted that day, but to no avail. The trout were apparently just not interested in eating. I finally abandoned them in frustration, just as the other anglers obviously had earlier in the day.

Nimblewill still can provide some interesting outings to the angler who approaches it imaginatively. One year I decided to open the season on a heavily stocked and fished stream just to remind myself of what a circus the event can be. The creek I settled on for the experiment was Nimblewill.

As expected, virtually every parking spot was taken, the smells of fresh campfires and cooking food permeated the air, and the angling hordes were on the creek banks in force. I had planned to fish upstream with dry flies, but soon discovered this to be impractical. Literally every pool and run on the creek had one or two bait anglers posted on it. As soon as one person left, the position was almost immediately filled by someone else. Unless I wanted to be brazen enough to float my flies over the baited lines, I needed a new approach.

The salvation for my morning of fishing came in the form of a tiny brook that entered the main stem of Nimblewill from the northwest side of the creek. Since I was unable to fish the main creek correctly, I began dropping my flies onto the surface of the small pools and potholes of this mini-creek, as a way to get away from the crowd.

Though the stream was so small that it could be jumped across without much effort, I found that each undercut bank or bubbling hole at the foot of a waterfall held fish. Working about a mile up this tributary, I caught and released a dozen fish in the 8- to 9-inch range and, of course, had the brook to myself. Among the fish I landed was one 9-inch male rainbow that had a head the size you would expect to find on a much larger fish, complete with the upturned lower lip of a kipped jaw that is found on older mature male trout.

Apparently this wild fish had lived several years in this brook where the food sources were not adequate to supply its needs. In fact, none of the rainbows I caught that day had ever seen the inside of a hatchery. They carried the rich, vivid colors of stream-reared trout. Yet they had managed to remain overlooked and unfished only a stone's throw from one of the Blue Ridge WMA's most visited streams. It always pays to approach each stream with an open mind.

Access to Nimblewill Creek is good, with getting there often being easier than finding a parking spot. FS 28-2 parallels the creek, often in sight of the bank. From GA 52 west of Dahlonega, turn north onto the paved section of FS 28 beside Grizzles Store. After a few miles this road forks, with FS 28-2 going to the left, and changing to gravel. Continue onto the Blue Ridge WMA and the creek is on the right.

JONES CREEK
SIZE: *Small*
ACCESS: *Easy to moderate*
SPECIES: *Wild brown trout*
SPECIAL REGULATIONS: *Artificial lures only*

Jones Creek is located to the east and slightly north of Nimblewill. This small stream is one of the more unusual creeks in the WMA system in that it is managed as a wild brown trout fishery. No stocking takes place, and fishing is limited to artificial lures only. This regulation applies to all of Jones Creek's feeder streams on the WMA as well.

The trout in this drainage run from 6 to 12 inches, are extremely colorful, and are very difficult to catch. Brown trout have the reputation of being the wariest fish in Georgia's trout waters, and in Jones Creek they earn that reputation.

Particularly during late summer and fall—periods of low, clear water—it is often necessary to downsize your lures to 1/32-ounce spinners and flies as small as Nos. 16 to 18. When casting spinners it is sometimes necessary to cast upstream to the next pool to get a shot at these fish. Under any circumstances, stalking is especially important on Jones Creek.

The brown trout's tendency to be very wary does have its advantage. Anglers are almost assured of there being some good fish in Jones Creek at any time of the year. Since browns are fall spawners and get much more aggressive at that time of the year, Jones is a good choice for fishing late in the season.

In fact, trout of up to 12 inches sometimes appear right in the middle of the most popular camping areas at this time of year, in spite of being in water that takes a pounding from anglers throughout the season.

When fishing spinners in the creek, black often has proven to be a good color. This may be because the brownies are fond of the small black spring lizards that inhabit the creek.

Fishing pressure is very light on Jones during the week, but picks up each weekend. The stream has a following of regular anglers, but they usually do not all show up at once, except on opening day or on holiday weekends.

Directions for finding Jones Creek begin the same as for Nimblewill. However, a couple of miles up FS 28 on its paved section, a gravel road marked FS 28-1 forks off sharply to the right. Follow this road for a couple of miles, crossing Jones Creek. A little farther up 28-1, Winding Stair Road (FS 77) enters from the left. Take FS 77 and follow it for a short distance and turn left again onto a spur (FS 77A) that is marked with a sign for Jones Creek. The spur leads to a primitive camping area on the mid-portion of the stream.

ETOWAH RIVER
Size: *Small*
Access: *Easy to Moderate*
Species: *Stocked and wild brown and rainbow trout*

The headwaters of the Etowah River are also found on the Blue Ridge WMA. The river flows in a southeasterly direction and exits the management area at the bridge under FS 28-1. On the upstream side of FS 28-1, where the river leaves the WMA, a short dirt road parallels the stream giving access to a string of primitive campgrounds along the shore. The gentle grade of the streambed and enticing pools of the flow in this section make it a favorite for family camping.

Unfortunately, the campers are not always kind to the area, and it tends to be rather trashy. On occasion scout troops or Trout Unlimited volunteers clean the area up, but it never seems to stay that way for long.

With the crowd of campers at the lower edge of the WMA, as might be expected, the Etowah attracts heavy fishing pressure. To accommodate these anglers, the creek receives heavy stockings of catchable-sized rainbow trout in the 8- to 10-inch range. From opening day on through the summer, the creek will often be crowded with bait casters up to the head of the camping area or slightly above it.

Away from the spur road and its campsites, the number of anglers plummets. About a half-mile upstream, at the first set of major shoals and small waterfalls, is the upper limit of where the stocked fish are found. Above this point the Etowah, and, to an even greater extent, its tributary the West Fork of Montgomery Creek, take on a very different character.

Because the river is accessible only by foot travel through this section, the wild trout found here go unmolested for most of the season. Although many of the fish run about 7 to 8 inches in length, an experienced angler can find fish of 10 inches or larger fairly regularly. The creek supports a population that is predominantly made up of rainbow trout, but some browns are present.

The main stem of the Etowah has a rather large waterfall and a big pool a bit farther upstream, and above this point it runs through the US Army's Frank Merrill Ranger Training Camp. The creek is small above the falls and not worth the effort to fish, especially because of the risk of walking into the middle of a ranger training exercise. You may be surprised by low-flying helicopters anywhere on the stream as they head for the camp.

Finding the WMA portion of the Etowah River can be difficult if you are asking directions. On occasions it is referred to locally as Montgomery Creek or by its older name, the Hightower River. To locate the headwaters of the Etowah, follow the directions for Jones Creek, but stay on FS 28-1 past the intersection with Winding Stair Road (FS 77). A couple of more miles brings you to another intersection at which you need to bear to the left to stay on FS 28-1. Continue driving and cross the bridge over the river. The spur road into the campsites is on the left immediately beyond the bridge.

WEST FORK OF MONTGOMERY CREEK
SIZE: *Small*
ACCESS: *Difficult*
SPECIES: *Wild brown and rainbow trout*

The final stream to be covered on the Blue Ridge WMA is the West Fork of Montgomery Creek. This is another creek that suffers from a bit of an identity crisis. Some older local residents still refer to it as Black's Creek.

A short way above the first shoals that were mentioned on the Etowah earlier, two small brooks only a few feet apart enter the river from the west. So small that they usually go unnoticed by the few anglers who venture this far up the river, these brooks are actually both part of the West Fork of Montgomery Creek, which splits here to flow around a small island. Even on the upstream side of the island, however, the slow-moving stream is not very big.

Again, the size of the West Fork camouflages its potential. The persevering explorer will begin to run into some spectacular waterfalls and deep, inviting pools and runs. The stream actually seems to get larger farther up the creek, and the fishing gets better as well. This stretch of water has rewarded my efforts with a higher percentage of 10-inch and bigger wild fish than any other small stream in the mountains.

It is open enough for fly-fishing through most of its course and the fish will readily take a dry fly under normal circumstances. That is not to say that the fishing is easy or always good; the terrain is rather rugged on the West Fork, and the fish can be temperamental. There are no guarantees in fishing!

One reason for the above-average angling on the West Fork is that the water is also deep in some runs, giving larger fish a spot to live and grow old. I was once fishing this branch and tried to skirt a pool at the bottom of a small waterfall after fishing the hole. Moving along the left side of the pool, I had to cut across a slanted, moss-covered rock or else climb the steep ravine wall to get around the rock.

As I edged along the slippery face, naturally, I lost my footing. Rather than struggling against the inevitable, I simply let myself slide down into the water. After all, it was a hot day, and I was wading wet. How deep could the water be in this small stream? Soon enough I learned the answer to that question, as I plunged into icy water that was about 8 feet deep. It is amazing how much gear you can carry in a fly vest that will float away when you go underwater. It is also astoundingly hard to catch that gear as it drifts away downstream.

In spite of its scenery and fishing, the West Fork of Montgomery Creek receives very little angling pressure. This is due in large part to the mile or two of hiking that is required along the Etowah River to reach the area from FS 28-1. The headwaters can be approached over a dirt road marked on the maps as FS 141, which cuts off FS 28-1 farther north, but a downstream hike is still required to get to the better waters.

CHAPTER FOURTEEN

Coopers Creek WMA

Situated on 30,000 acres of land, all of which is owned by the US Forest Service, Coopers Creek WMA spreads across sections of Fannin and Union counties. Although the management area contains some rugged, mountainous terrain, the trout streams in the WMA have fairly easy access.

Cooper Creek and its two main tributaries, Mulky and Sea creeks, provide virtually all of the fishing opportunities available on the WMA. Also located within the management area is the Cooper Creek Scenic Area, which the Forest Service oversees. (Note that the spellings "Cooper Creek" and "Coopers Creek" are used here as they appear most frequently in official sources.)

COOPER CREEK
SIZE: *Small to medium*
ACCESS: *Easy to moderate*
SPECIES: *Stocked and wild brown and rainbow trout*

Not only the namesake stream of the WMA, Cooper Creek is also the only major watershed on this reserve. Rising at the foot of the dam on Lake Winfield Scott at the eastern edge of the management area, the stream cuts a swath through the middle of the WMA flowing westerly to its junction with Toccoa River.

Coopers Creek WMA

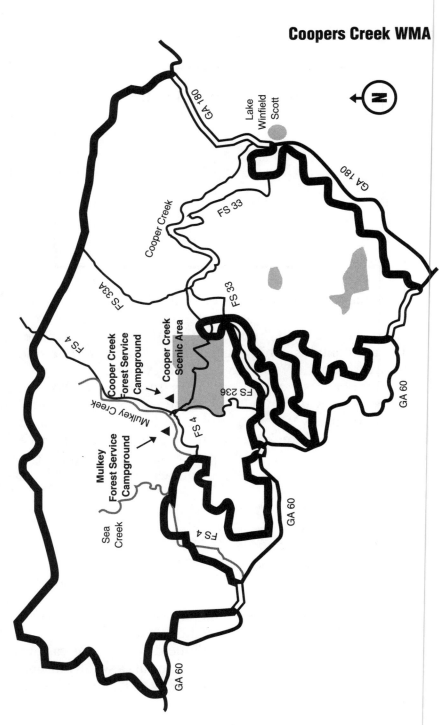

Cooper Creek could well be termed the "Dr. Jekyll and Mr. Hyde" destination of Georgia trout fishing. It has two very distinct personalities as far as water conditions and accessibility are concerned.

From its junction with the Toccoa just east of Deep Hole, Cooper Creek's lower 4 miles from GA 60 up to the edge of the WMA near the mouth of Mulky Creek often appear pastoral in nature. Running through open fields alongside FS 4, the creek is the very picture of mountain serenity. As to access, it flows virtually through the backyards of several farm houses and cabins. Although this part of the creek looks like terrific water, it cannot be approached without permission of the owners of the farms and cabins.

At one time back in the early 1970s, the portion of the creek immediately above GA 60 had a streamside sign proclaiming it private property, but also giving permission to the public to fish as long as the anglers did not litter the stream. Sadly, public fishing is no longer allowed here. Undoubtedly our collective disregard for the beauty of the creek banks and the landowner's desire to keep the stream clean cost us the privilege of fishing there.

Now the only tame portions of the creek that are still available to the general public are the several hundred yards above the southern boundary of the wildlife management area. These portions surround the Mulky and Cooper Creek Forest Service campgrounds, which give the WMA a reputation as a good place for family outings. Convenient access to the road allows the use of large tents, campers, and motor homes.

Through here the stream is big and offers some deeper pools to entice the visiting angler. As you can imagine, on opening day or any weekend during the spring and summer months, the area around the campgrounds gets heavy fishing pressure. Particularly early in the season, this is the land of elbow-to-elbow angling. The situation is great for camaraderie and an abundance of stocked fish, but lacks the solitude and aesthetics usually associated with trout fishing.

To support this pressure the creek is stocked regularly with brown and rainbow trout throughout the season along its entire length. As with most stocked streams there are some wild trout present as well.

Above the campgrounds, however, the nature of the stream begins to change. The road veers away from the creek's course, and the terrain becomes steeper. The beauty of this wild and remote section has little in common with the area downstream. This is also the location of the Cooper Creek Scenic Area and the trail that bears the same name, as well as the beginning of the rough-and-tumble portion of the creek that provides the "scenic" part of the moniker.

From the parking lot for the Cooper Creek Scenic Area upstream, the creek is rougher and less accessible, and wild trout become more common. Some of the small feeder streams of this upper portion even continue to harbor wild native brook trout. All access to the middle section of the stream is by foot travel. Farther up, FS 33 and 33-A provide points of road access to the headwaters of Cooper Creek. Several tributaries such as Mat Helton, Bryant and Barnett creeks, which harbor some wild trout, enter the upper portion of the main branch, but these are small, inaccessible, and bushy brooklets.

To get to Cooper Creek's lower section take either FS 4, off GA 60 near Deep Hole on the Toccoa River, or FS 236 that is farther east on GA 60. This latter road runs northward to intersect FS 4 at the campgrounds on the creek.

For the headwaters of the creek above the Scenic Area, FS 33 runs off of FS 236 in an easterly direction not far north of GA 60. Be aware that FS 33 is marked as 163 on some maps of the area, but signs on the road itself identify it by its 33 designation. From its intersection with FS 33A, this gravel road parallels upper Cooper Creek for several miles.

MULKY CREEK
Size: *Small*
Access: *Easy*
Species: *Wild brown and rainbow trout*

Mulky Creek is a small tributary that is a major feeder stream on the lower part of Cooper Creek. It is about one-third the size of Cooper and is quite overgrown and not easily fished. Entering Cooper Creek from the north, Mulky receives no stocking and much less fishing pressure than does the larger stream. Although the creek contains wild rainbows, Mulky will also give up a brown trout of more than 10 inches from time to time. To reach Mulky Creek stay on FS 4 when it turns north away from Cooper Creek between the two Forest Service campgrounds. This gravel road parallels the stream's course for several miles.

SEA CREEK
Size: *Small*
Access: *Easy*
Species: *Wild rainbow trout*

Sea Creek is a small feeder stream that enters Cooper Creek below the Mulky Campground. It contains a population of wild trout, composed mostly of small rainbows. Although too small to be discussed as a major destination, Sea Creek is mentioned because of its prominent location where most anglers see it on their way into or out of Cooper Creek, and because it has some primitive camping areas along its lower section. These campsites often catch the overflow when the Forest Service campgrounds on Cooper Creek are full.

The brook is crossed by FS 4, and a dirt spur runs north from the Forest Service road along Sea Creek for a distance.

Local Trout Unlimited chapters have done some stream renovation and in-stream structure work on the first couple of
hundred yards of water above the road and have greatly
improved the habitat on that section, which is open to the
public. The creek is on private land below the bridge over FS 4.

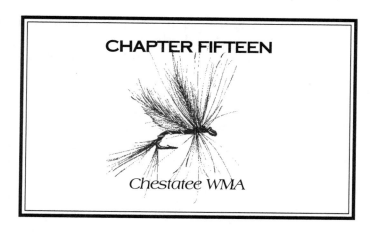

CHAPTER FIFTEEN

Chestatee WMA

The Chestatee WMA is located in north-central Georgia in Lumpkin and White counties. It covers roughly 25,000 acres of rugged, mountainous terrain that is predominantly owned by the US Forest Service. There are, however, some small private tracts of land on lower Dicks Creek and below DeSoto Falls on Frogtown Creek.

The northern boundary of the WMA is formed by the Appalachian Trail as it follows the crest of the mountains from Woody Gap through Neels Gap to the Richard Russell Scenic Highway (GA 348). The streams here all flow to the south and are feeders of the Chestatee River.

In spite of the steep mountains and generally rough terrain, the creeks on this WMA tend to be quite accessible. Most are close to paved roads and can be reached with very minimal driving on gravel tracks.

DICKS CREEK
SIZE: *Small to Large*
ACCESS: *Easy*
SPECIES: *Stocked and wild brown and rainbow trout*

Dicks Creek is the main tributary—or, more correctly, headwater—of the Chestatee River. It rises in the western segment of the WMA, and all of the fishable trout water in the area is found within its watershed.

The name of the this creek can be a source of some confusion, because it is a name that reappears on other creeks on other WMAs. When it comes to our trout streams, sometimes you need a map to tell which creek is which. The names Dicks, Rough, and Rock creeks were all popular with the folks who named Georgia's trout waters. In the case of Dicks Creek, the one that is best known and most often referred to is on the Chestatee WMA.

Dicks Creek runs the gamut from being a small, high-altitude brook in its headwaters to becoming a large, open creek just before it is joined by Boggs Creek to form the main stem of the Chestatee River. Although the stream receives heavy stockings of hatchery rainbows during the trout season, it still will produce a surprising number of wild fish in certain areas.

Upstream in the headwaters, many brightly colored little wild rainbows can be found. Also, the area just upstream of the junction of Dicks and Waters creeks also produces an inordinate number of wild fish. This part of the stream wanders away from the parallel gravel road and flows through a bit of a ravine that includes a waterfall of perhaps 25 feet that necessitates getting out of the stream to walk around. These factors, of course, are a prescription for an area to hold wild trout. A portion that is hard to fish and requires the angler to walk a couple of hundred yards to it will have enough less fishing pressure to allow such a population to survive.

Another surprising fact about the fishery in Dicks Creek is the number of large trout that turn up in it each year. Every season, three or four fish of 20 inches or better are caught from Dicks Creek. Some of these, which are landed in the lower reaches of the stream on the WMA below the Waters Creek junction, may be accounted for by migration of fish downstream out of the latter creek's trophy fishery.

The upstream area, however, also produces some trophy fish. Several seasons back a brown of almost 30 inches that weighed less than 5 pounds was taken from tiny Blood Mountain Creek that feeds into Dicks Creek. It was a fish that, for its age and length, should have weighed more, but undoubtedly it had remained slender because there was not enough food in such a small brook to fatten it up. There are enough large falls on Dicks Creek's midsection to make upstream migration an unlikely explanation for the presence of the larger fish in headwaters areas.

If you favor catching a stringer of stockers to eat and still have the hope of landing a bragging fish, Dicks Creek is the place. Most of the middle to lower sections of Dicks are open enough for fly-fishing, though the vast majority of anglers use bait. There will usually be no shortage of these anglers, either. Dicks Creek gets heavy fishing pressure on weekends throughout the season and ranks in the top two or three most popular creeks for trout in Georgia.

The area downstream of the Waters Creek confluence attracts a lot of swimmers when the weather is warm. Near the Dicks Creek Falls, particularly, bathers will often be present in large enough numbers to restrict or prevent fishing the area.

The Forest Service's Waters Creek Campground is located at streamside on the lower portion of Dicks Creek. Be aware that there is some private, posted land in both directions from this camping area. Farther upstream, above the junction with Waters Creek, there are a number of primitive camping sites available along the creek on public land.

Access to the creek is good via Waters Creek Road (FS 34) from US 19, just west of Turners Corner. Waters Creek Road is paved all the way to where its namesake creek joins Dicks Creek. A gravel road shown on the maps as FS 34-1 continues upstream along Dicks Creek from that point.

To get to Waters Creek Road, take GA 60 north out of Dahlonega to Stone Pile Gap. Bear right on US 19 and watch for Waters Creek Road on the left at 7 miles.

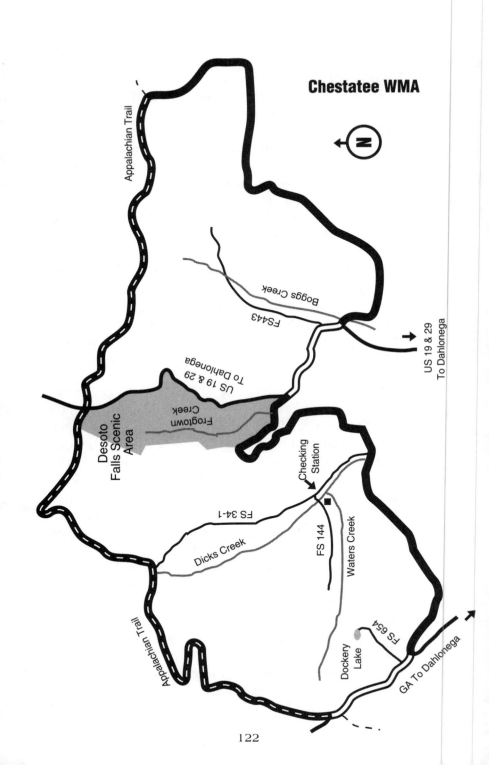

Chestatee WMA

WATERS CREEK

SIZE: *Small*
ACCESS: *Easy*
SPECIES: *Stocked brook and brown trout, wild rainbow trout*
SPECIAL REGULATIONS: *Artificial lures only, trophy trout restrictions*

For anglers who want to take a truly large trout from a small stream, Waters Creek is hard to beat anywhere else in the Southeast. For almost two decades the creek has been managed jointly by the Georgia Game and Fish Division, the US Fish and Wildlife Service, and Georgia Trout Unlimited as a trophy-trout fishery with some quite stringent regulations on angling methods. Only artificial lures with single, barbless hooks of No. 6 or smaller are allowed, and landing nets cannot exceed 2 feet in length. A creel limit of one fish per day (to a maximum of three fish per season for a single angler) with a minimum size of 18 inches for brook trout and 22 inches for rainbow and browns is in effect. Anglers must check in and out of the stream at the checking station, and fishing hours are from 30 minutes before sunrise until 6:30 EST (7:30 EDT) on Wednesdays, Saturdays, and Sundays during the regular trout season (the last weekend of March through the end of October).

In addition to the state fishing license and trout stamp, a Wildlife Management Area Stamp is required before fishing. These are not sold at the check station and must all be acquired in advance.

In spite of this plethora of rules, which apply to all of the stream's feeder waters as well, Waters Creek was rated as a heavily fished stream up until 1988, when a much-publicized poaching incident scared many anglers away. Just before the 1988 season opened, a band of backwoods hoodlums struck the stream and gigged or netted as many as 100 trout of more than 20 inches. In spite of thousands of dollars of rewards offered by the state and Trout Unlimited, no one was ever charged with the crime. The immediate effect was a drop in numbers of anglers on the stream, plus a drop in numbers of keeper trout from 76 in 1987 to only 3 in 1988, with another 10 to 12 reported caught and released that year.

During the preceding heavily fished years, the 2.5 miles of water on the stream produced some astounding angling results. Through the 1980s the number of keeper fish checked out increased each year until the 76 taken in 1987. Most were rainbows in excess of 22 inches, but rainbows up to 12 pounds, browns up to 9 pounds, and brook trout pushing 5 pounds have been caught from Waters Creek. Some stocking of browns and brookies is done each year, but only fish of 10 to 14 inches are introduced so that they have time to grow up and get wild before being taken out as trophies.

Although the rainbow population is self-sustaining, the trophy sizes the fish reach are the result of the angling regulations and a supplemental feeding program. Several times a week food pellets are released into the creek to promote faster growth and larger fish.

As with Noontootla on the Blue Ridge WMA, one of the prerequisites for establishing Waters Creek as a managed stream was its location in the protected confines of a WMA completely in the Chattahoochee National Forest. Located about 20 miles north of Dahlonega, this entire watershed is on public land.

Although the poaching incident hurt the trophy fishing, regular anglers and biologists noted that by 1989 catch rates were improving on the stream. The number of anglers has dropped because of the adverse publicity, but those who do show up have reported that the number of 15- to 20-inch trout caught and released is up significantly.

There are actually two ways to approach the fishing on Waters Creek. The standard method involves going after the big trout in the creek, which is to say strictly trophy fishing. This is, of course, the reason the stream management project was established. Trophy angling calls for some specialized tactics that we will discuss shortly.

The second method that can be employed, especially on days when the fishing pressure is light, is to fish Waters Creek the same as any other stream. In other words, target the smaller fish. Using this method, an angler will find plenty of trout in the 8- to 12-inch range, will have a shot at catching fish up to 20 inches, and will see some of the behemoths of up to 26 inches in a number of pools. These largest trout, however, are very difficult to entice.

On one particular trip to Waters Creek, Don Pfitzer and I arrived on the stream to discover one pool that had some trout actively feeding on the surface. This pool was in a bend in the creek with the current sweeping along a log inset in one bank.

The fish were apparently lying in the undercut area beneath the log and darting up to catch insects on the surface. In the low, early morning light, we could not actually make out the outline of the fish, but their rises were consistent and often quite splashy.

We slipped across the creek well upstream and, stooping, crawling, and duck-walking, worked our way down to a position beside the pool from which it was possible to cast to the fish. Watching the rises for a moment or two we saw that the insects that were attracting the action were very tiny and of a pale, almost white, hue.

I watched Don cast various dry-fly patterns to these trout, but to no avail. He then insisted that I move forward and give them a try. In a short time I also had tossed my complete collection of light-colored insect imitations at the rises without getting a strike. Not being an overly patient angler, I moved off upstream to look for more willing quarry, leaving the still-feeding fish to Mr. Pfitzer.

A few pools upstream I hooked and landed a respectable, richly colored, 12-inch rainbow, which scratched my angling itch enough that I could return to see how Don was faring. I found him still crouched by the original pool, continuing cautiously to drop an array of flies on or into the water. He had now branched out to include wet flies and nymphs in his offerings as well. The result of his intense concentration on this pool of active feeding fish was the hooking and releasing of a single fish that was only in the 10-inch range.

The conclusion of this story is that, returning to the pool in the afternoon when the sun was penetrating the water from a sharper angle, we stood on the overlooking bank and could see a pod of almost a dozen trout in the 18- to 24-inch range lying in the spot we had fished. Yet we had tried all our standard tactics on them when they were on an active feed and could not interest them!

Targeting the large trout in Waters Creek calls for some specialized techniques. The serious trophy seekers can be spotted by their full-camouflage attire in a forest-green pattern. This is the preferred uniform of the day, in that remaining invisible to the big trout is a necessity.

These anglers also refrain from wading the stream except when it is absolutely necessary in order to cross it. The less the water is disturbed, the better the chances are of sneaking up on magnum trout.

Finally, the bulk of the big fish caught from Waters Creek fall victim to small, minnow-like spinners or to a "cork" fly. The latter is an imitation of the food pellets that are released into the stream as supplemental feed. This lure is basically a piece of tan or brown cork tied to a small hook and dead-drifted downstream through a pool where a big fish has been spotted.

The angler using either spinner or cork will usually arrive very early, will be concealed beside a targeted pool when the legal fishing begins, and will offer the lure or fly to the fish periodically in a manner designed not to let the fish see it too often. Such a battle of wits can go on for hours. Usually the fish win, but occasionally the angler's patience will be rewarded with a rainbow, brown, or brookie of gargantuan proportions.

This type of fishing obviously is not for everyone, and the trophy anglers, many of whom are regulars to the stream and fish specific pools on an equally regular basis, do not take kindly to having people wade in front of them or come strolling carelessly up the creek bank.

The rangers at the checking station tell of a woman who fished virtually every weekend using these trophy tactics. On one particular Saturday she checked in early and disappeared upstream. A bit later a fellow showed up, who, at best, would be described as a novice. This noisy newcomer was outfitted with completely new fishing gear, had on a white shirt that probably spooked some fish when he got out of his car, and asked questions of the rangers that made it obvious he had never before fished for trout.

After confidently plying the ranger on duty for a little information on where and how to fish, the man walked down to the creek behind the station, plunged into the stream, and began sloshing up the middle of it.

Within half an hour the novice angler was back at the station to pick up his license, but he was now subdued and quiet and seemed anxious to get out of there. The ranger noticed that he also looked a little flushed as he hurried back to his car and drove away

Not long after that, the woman mentioned at the beginning of the story showed up at the checking station appearing rather embarrassed. She explained that she had staked out one of her favorite pools in which she had spotted and was casting to a keeper-sized trout. Naturally, her senses were on edge each time she carefully presented her offering.

At this moment our novice angler came trudging out into her pool with a loud shout that he was just passing though and asking had she caught anything? Apologizing to the ranger, the woman admitted that she had lost her cool, leaped into the water, and attacked the intruder with both her tongue and her fly rod, causing him to beat a hasty retreat back downstream.

Streamside etiquette is important on all trout waters, and failure to observe it can be downright confrontational on Water Creek, or anywhere else trophy fish are sought. Anyone using standard fishing tactics on a creek, should be aware of other anglers and give them a wide berth if they are already on a pool.

Fishing pressure on Waters Creek can be moderate on weekends but will usually be light on Wednesdays. Mid-week will at times find fewer than ten anglers on the stream.

One innovation that has helped to lessen the pressure is the institution of the regulation requiring a Wildlife Management Area Stamp in order to fish. The stamp costs $19.00 and must be purchased from a sporting goods outlet or bait shop where fishing licenses are sold before arriving at the creek.

Directions for Waters Creek are the same as for Dicks Creek. At the junction of Dicks and Waters creeks, turn left over the bridge across Dicks Creek and follow gravel FS 144 to the checking station. From there, the road continues to parallel Waters Creek for most of its length.

DOCKERY LAKE

    SIZE: *Large*
    ACCESS: *Easy*
    SPECIES: *Stocked rainbow trout*

Dockery Lake is a bit of an oddity when it comes to Georgia mountain trout angling. It is a small pond that is stocked with trout, and fishing is allowed only during the regular trout season.

Located on a feeder stream of Waters Creek, the lake is exempt from the special regulations imposed on that stream and its tributaries. Trophy regulations are in effect, however, immediately below the spillway of the lake.

Catchable-sized rainbow trout are stocked in the lake regularly during the spring and summer. The bulk of the fishing done on the lake is with bait and occasionally with spinners cast from shore.

Access is easy to Dockery Lake via FS 654 from GA 60. The intersection of these two roads is about 3 miles north of Stone Pile Gap, with FS 654 entering GA 60 from the right.

The Forest Service maintains the Dockery Lake Campground on the shores of the lake. Both the camping facilities and the lake experience moderate to heavy usage during the entire spring and summer seasons.

FROGTOWN CREEK
SIZE: *Small*
ACCESS: *Easy*
SPECIES: *Stocked and wild rainbow trout*

Another of the tributary streams that make up the headwaters of the Chestatee River, Frogtown is mentioned more for its location than its angling possibilities. It is a small creek that flows through the Forest Service's Desoto Falls Campground, putting many people on its banks each season.

The creek is stocked occasionally with rainbow trout, but it also contains some wild fish as well. Because of its size, Frogtown would not be a major destination stream, but one to sample when camping at Desoto Falls. Although there are plenty of campers in the area throughout the season, fishing pressure on the stream does not appear to be overly heavy.

To get to the creek and the Desoto Falls Scenic Area, take US 19/129 north from Turners Corner. Watch for the campground sign on the left of the road.

BOGGS CREEK
SIZE: *Small*
ACCESS: *Easy*
SPECIES: *Stocked and wild brown and rainbow trout*

Boggs Creek is a small flow that eventually empties into Dicks Creek to form the Chestatee River. Stocked sporadically with catchable-sized rainbow trout, the creek also holds a population of large brown trout that feed on the stockers. My experience on Boggs, however, has produced mostly small, wild rainbows and browns under 10 inches. Some stocked rainbows have turned up, but the big browns have yet to make an appearance while I have been on the stream.

Access is easy to most of Boggs Creek via FS 443, which is a gravel road running off of US 19/129. Traveling north from Turners Corner, US 19/129 crosses Boggs Creek at 1.5 miles. The Forest Service road is on the right just beyond the bridge. A WMA boundary sign is located a short distance down FS 443.

Boggs Creek appears to get moderate to heavy fishing pressure, especially when word spreads that the hatchery trucks have just visited the stream. A number of primitive campsites are located along its lower stretches, and many will be in use on the average spring or summer weekend.

Most anglers on Boggs Creek fish with bait, but the number of brown trout present suggests that spinners would be another good choice, particularly for larger fish.

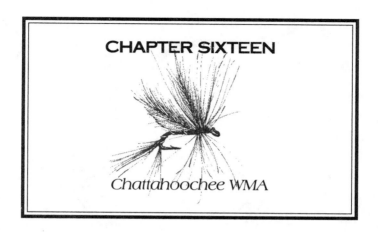

CHAPTER SIXTEEN

Chattahoochee WMA

The Chattahoochee Wildlife Management Area is located in the northeastern part of the state, just a few miles northwest of Georgia's alpine resort town of Helen. Situated in some very mountainous and rugged terrain, the WMA consists of 24,000 acres of US Forest Service land in Union, Towns, and White counties.

All of the streams on the WMA flow in a southeasterly direction and are headwaters or tributaries of the Chattahoochee River. The general vicinity of the WMA around Helen can become quite busy during peak vacation periods of the summer and during the annual pilgrimage of metro Atlantans to the mountains for the changing of the leaves in October. While not having a particularly large impact on fishing pressure on the WMA, the crowds can make travel to the area a problem at times.

In spite of high mountains and steep hillsides, overall access to the three major trout streams of the Chattahoochee WMA is very good. Forest Service roads or paved highways make the streams fairly easy to reach.

One interesting feature of the Chattahoochee WMA is the presence of trout checking stations as well as the hunting

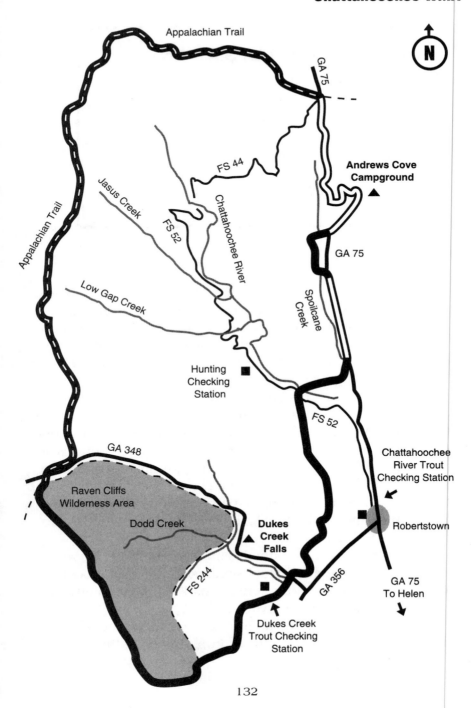

Chattahoochee WMA

N

Appalachian Trail

GA 75

Andrews Cove
Campground

FS 44

Jasus Creek

Appalachian Trail

FS 52

Chattahoochee River

GA 75

Spoilcane
Creek

Low Gap Creek

Hunting
Checking
Station

FS 52

GA 348

Chattahoochee
River Trout
Checking Station

Raven Cliffs
Wilderness Area

Dodd Creek

Dukes
Creek
Falls

Robertstown

FS 244

GA 356

GA 75
To Helen

Dukes Creek
Trout Checking
Station

checking stations found on most WMAs. One of these trout stations is found at the GA 356 bridge over the Chattahoochee River at Robertstown, and the other is on Dukes Creek, just upstream of where it crosses GA 356. These are relics of earlier years when the WMA was much more heavily managed as the trout fishery was being developed. Checking in and out of the streams was then required of all anglers, along with creel checks. This is no longer the case, and the stations are used now only as bases of operations by the game wardens.

CHATTAHOOCHEE RIVER
SIZE: *Small to medium*
ACCESS: *Easy to moderate*
SPECIES: *Stocked and wild brook, brown, and rainbow trout*

The Chattahoochee River is, of course, the stream that gives the area its name and provides its major fishing resource. The portion of the river in the WMA is found along FS 52 to the northwest of Helen.

To a certain extent, this part of the Chattahoochee is overshadowed by the more popular fishing areas in the tailrace, many miles to the south. Yet, this portion of the river is not overlooked. It is a very popular primitive camping area, and the stream receives heavy angling attention. On opening day the fishing will be elbow-to-elbow, and this type of pressure occurs at other times of the season as well.

The Chattahoochee is a small to medium-sized stream on the WMA, but it is open enough to permit fly-fishing in its lower sections. Most of the fish encountered will be stocked rainbow and brown trout, but wild varieties of both are also found in the river. Above the falls at its junction with Henson Creek, the main branch of the Chattahoochee has been renovated as a habitat for wild brook trout. A thriving population of the reintroduced native brookies now exists in these headwaters.

The stocked trout in the Chattahoochee generally run from 8 to 11 inches, while the wild fish average only about 7 to 9 inches. The brookies in the headwaters will only be in the 5- to 7-inch range. There is, however, always the possibility of a larger trout, especially a brown, turning up in the lower reaches of the WMA waters.

One of the better areas for fishing traditionally has been located just above the hunting checking station near the eastern edge of the WMA on FS 52. At the point where the river runs away from the road and through a gorge, access is fairly difficult, and, as a result, there is less fishing pressure. Most of the bigger trout reported on the WMA come from this stretch.

Two of the feeder streams that empty into the Chattahoochee on the WMA support populations of trout and are worth mentioning. Both Low Gap and Jasus creeks enter the main river from the west in the gorge area and contain some wild rainbows of 6 to 9 inches. Neither stream is very big; however, they offer the opportunity to add some variety to a day or weekend of angling on the Chattahoochee. Both feeders are crossed by FS 52 as it follows the river upstream.

Access is possible all the way up to the Henson Creek junction via this same Forest Service road, but the going can be rough as it climbs toward the brook-trout waters. To reach FS 52, take GA 75 north out of Helen and turn left across the bridge onto GA 356 at Robertstown. Immediately after crossing the bridge, take the paved road to the right. This is FS 52, which parallels the river for a couple of miles before passing through a gate and changing to gravel. Watch for the wildlife management area boundary signs, as the road passes through some private land before reaching the WMA.

Another possibility for access to the upper stretches of the Chattahoochee is over FS 44, also off GA 75. FS 44 intersects GA 75 from the west, just south of Unicoi Gap.

DUKES CREEK
SIZE: *Small*
ACCESS: *Difficult*
SPECIES: *Wild rainbow trout*

Dukes Creek is a major tributary of the Chattahoochee River, but it does not empty into the river until both have exited the managed lands. Its watershed lies to the southwest of the Chattahoochee and runs roughly parallel to the river.

Dukes Creek is a rough-and-tumble stream that cascades down through a very picturesque area. A relatively small stream on the WMA, it is overlooked by most anglers, who prefer to concentrate on the larger Chattahoochee River. Part of this neglect can also be attributed to Dukes Creek's more difficult access.

The fish in Dukes Creek are exclusively wild trout, with rainbows making up most of the population. These trout run from 5 to 9 inches, but the creek is large enough and lightly enough fished to produce some bigger fish.

Dukes Creek is one of the more beautiful streams in the North Georgia mountains. Near its mid-point in the WMA it cascades through Duke Creek Falls, and there are several good-sized waterfalls on the main creek. The most impressive of the falls, however, is created where a tributary, Dodd Creek drops almost 100 feet down a rocky face to join Dukes Creek. A trail up Dodd Creek leads into the Raven Cliffs Wilderness Area, which is one of the more impressive natural areas of the Georgia mountains.

The mid-section of Dukes Creek, where it passes through the Dukes Creek Falls area, presents the greatest access challenge. There is a parking lot off of GA 348 for the falls and a 1 mile hiking trail down into the gorge through which the stream flows. The trail is a series of switchbacks and descends steeply.

As noted earlier, Dukes Creek is a relatively small stream. But because the bottom of the gorge is very rocky, the canopy of foliage is far enough back from the stream bank to make fly-fishing possible.

Fishing pressure on Dukes Creek is light overall. On the portion of the stream in the gorge around the falls, pressure appears to be almost nonexistent. Although from spring through fall there are virtually always cars in the parking area and people on the trail, they are almost exclusively sightseers and hikers. The sight of a fishing rod on the entrance trail is unusual.

On one recent May outing in the gorge I fished on a Saturday while enjoying excellent weather conditions. Although I had plenty of company traveling down the approach trail, I fished half a day encountering only hikers and one old-timer panning for gold below the falls. The only competition for space on the water likely will be found around the falls, where some of the sightseers will probably be wading to cool their feet before tackling the climb back out.

To reach Dukes Creek, take GA 356 west across the Chattahoochee River bridge from the intersection with GA 75 in Robertstown. At 2 miles, GA 348 enters from the right. Follow this road north, watching for the signs for Dukes Creek Falls on the left. A couple of miles farther up the highway, Dukes Creek passes under the road, and a dirt road (FS 244) turns off to the left just before the stream and leads to the head of the gorge above Dukes Creek Falls.

To reach the lower section of the creek, stay on GA 356 west through the intersection with GA 348. Just beyond the intersection there is a dirt road and sign for the checking station on the right. This road leads to the checking station and lower Dukes Creek.

SPOILCANE CREEK
Size: *Small*
Access: *Easy*
Species: *Stocked rainbow trout*

One last stream on the Chattahoochee WMA that deserves mention is Spoilcane Creek. This is another of the feeder streams that flows down to the Chattahoochee River. It is a small creek that merits inclusion because of its easy access. It flows immediately beside GA 75, skirting the eastern edge of the WMA, as that road runs north of Helen.

The stream flows through a mixture of private lands and public areas as it descends from Unicoi Gap. These various areas are fairly obvious and well marked. The creek is stocked with catchable-sized rainbow trout, and angling pressure appears to be surprisingly moderate considering the ready access to the stream.

To reach Spoilcane Creek, simply follow GA 75 north from Helen and watch for the creek on the left of the road after the highway leaves the Chattahoochee River.

CHAPTER SEVENTEEN

Swallow Creek WMA

Swallow Creek WMA is one of the lesser known and more difficult of the North Georgia management areas to fish. It is extremely rugged mountain terrain covering 19,000 acres of US Forest Service land in Towns County. The streams of the area are all tributaries of the Hiwassee River and flow generally to the northwest to form that river. Access to some of the creeks is good, but getting to others is quite strenuous.

Adding to the difficulty of fishing this area is the fact that three of the five trout streams on the WMA do not appear on the map in the "Guide To Georgia Trout Regulations" that is put out by the Department of Natural Resources. The missing streams (Swallow, Mill, and High Shoals creeks) are shown, however, on maps of the Swallow Creek WMA dispensed by the state, commercially available maps of the North Georgia WMAs, and the Forest Service maps of the Chattahoochee National Forest.

For the angler who wants to catch a limit of trout to cook for dinner, this WMA is probably a poor choice for a fishing destination. It is a haven for wild, stream-bred trout, and none of the creeks on the reserve is stocked with fish. If meat on the platter is the main concern, it will not be worth the effort required on the streams of this WMA.

Swallow Creek WMA's north-to-south axis is a long one, while it is rather narrow east to west. With this vertical configuration, most of the streams parallel each other in their race to the Hiwassee.

SWALLOW CREEK
SIZE: *Small*
ACCESS: *Easy to moderate*
SPECIES: *Wild rainbow trout*

Located on the extreme northern edge of the preserve, Swallow Creek eventually empties into Hightower Creek, which in turn joins the Hiwassee River in Lake Chatuge. The creek is a small flow that is heavily canopied with rhododendron, mountain laurel, and holly, making it fairly difficult to fish.

The predominant species of fish in Swallow Creek is the rainbow trout. For the most part, the fish run small, but vividly colored individuals of 8 to 9 inches turn up occasionally.

The first half mile of water on the stream near the western edge of the WMA has had some in-stream structures installed recently by Trout Unlimited. As a result the amount of holding water has increased and promises to improve the fishing.

From the west to Swallow Creek's lower section access is fairly easy over Swallow Creek Road (County Road 99), which is paved from US 76 to the edge of the WMA. Immediately upon entering the WMA the road, which appears on maps as FS 95 from the edge of the WMA, turns to gravel and fords the stream. This first ford is easily crossed by most passenger cars.

At a point 3/4 of a mile farther up the road the creek is forded again, but it is a more difficult crossing. The approaches from either side are a bit steep, and the water is somewhat deep, even at normal flow levels. It would be safer to try this one only with four-wheel drive vehicles. The road is less often used or maintained above the second ford, but it

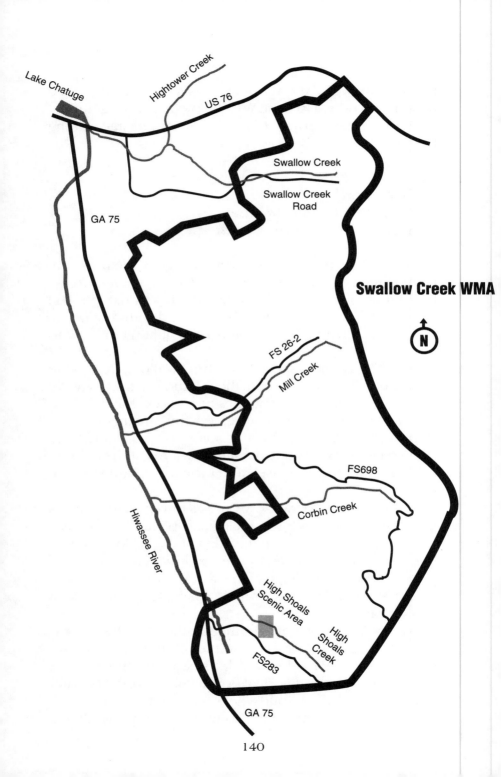

Lake Chatuge

Hightower Creek

US 76

Swallow Creek

Swallow Creek
Road

GA 75

Swallow Creek WMA

N

FS 26-2

Mill Creek

FS698

Corbin Creek

Hiwassee River

High Shoals
Scenic Area

High
Shoals
Creek

FS283

GA 75

does parallel the stream in the form of a rough track all the way to the headwaters of the creek.

There is a wildlife clearing just before the second ford that offers a good parking area. Beyond this ford a number of primitive camping sites are located between the road and creek. The in-stream structure mentioned earlier is beside and downstream of the clearing.

To find Swallow Creek, take GA 75 north from Helen to the intersection with US 76. Turn right, proceed to Swallow Creek Road, and turn right again for the final approach to the WMA. A sign for Lower Hightower Baptist Church appears at the intersection of US 76 and Swallow Creek Road, and the church itself is on the right after the turn. It is 1.8 miles to the end of the pavement and the edge of the Swallow Creek WMA.

MILL CREEK

Size: *Small to medium*
Access: *Easy to moderate*
Species: *Wild brown and rainbow trout*

The next stream encountered moving south is Mill Creek. This is another popular name for Georgia trout water, and both the Cohutta and Coleman River WMAs have similarly named flows.

This edition of Mill Creek feeds directly into the Hiwassee River and is probably the most popular of the trout streams on the Swallow Creek WMA. It is a bit larger than the area's other creeks, especially in its lower reaches where access is fairly easy. These two facts undoubtedly account for its popularity.

As with Swallow Creek, wild rainbow trout will dominate the stream, but some browns are also present. Similar to other streams on this WMA, Mill Creek is not blessed with an abundance of holding water. It goes through shallow, swift stretches that are broader than they are deep.

The stream is followed for its entire length on the WMA lands by a Forest Service road, which is designated FS 26-2 on maps of the area. The small sign at the beginning of the gravel part of the road, however, is marked simply as 26. The road meanders up onto the mountainside after running along the creek for a short way. Above this point of departure, access to the stream is more difficult.

To locate Mill Creek, take GA 75 north from Helen. After 75 crosses the Hiwassee River the first time, begin watching for Mill Creek Road on the right. There is a sign at the intersection identifying this paved road. (If you get to a second bridge over the Hiwassee on GA 75, you will know that you have missed Mill Creek Road.)

Turn right on Mill Creek Road and proceed east for 1.1 miles, at which point FS 26-2 runs sharply uphill to the left. This gravel road goes over the shoulder of the hillside and into a valley before Mill Creek appears on the right side of the road. The creek is on public land upstream from this point.

CORBIN CREEK
Size: *Small to medium*
Access: *Difficult*
Species: *Wild brown and rainbow trout*

Corbin Creek is by far the most difficult to reach and fish of the streams on the Swallow Creek area. For much of its length it flows through a gorge that can require a couple of hours of walking in order to reach its lower end. The only portion that is easily accessible by road is the very headwaters, where the creek is quite small.

The Corbin Creek gorge has a reputation for both good trout fishing and abundant timber rattlesnakes, though I have not personally encountered the latter of these slithering residents. The pools on the creek are short but deep, and, because of their location, they obviously do not get a lot of fishing pressure. Be aware that you are a long way from help when you venture onto slick rocks of the gorge among these pools.

As with the other streams on the WMA, Corbin Creek is

not presently stocked with hatchery fish. Rainbow and brown trout will both be found in the creek.

To locate Corbin Creek, travel north from Helen on GA 75 until you cross the Hiwassee River for the first time. Immediately across the bridge, FS 698 is on the right. This road runs along the edge of the gorge until it finally hits the creek well up in the mountains. Note that there is some private, posted land on Corbin Creek's lower segment near its junction with the Hiwassee River.

There are some clearings for primitive camping along the headwaters of the creek where the road finally strikes it. An old trail suitable for hiking also descends along the creek from this upstream area.

HIWASSEE RIVER
SIZE: *Small*
ACCESS: *Easy*
SPECIES: *Wild rainbow trout*

Unfortunately, it is hard not to be disappointed by the public-access portion of the Hiwassee River. From GA 75 northward along its valley, the river appears almost constantly as a large, tantalizing trout stream weaving in and out of farms and resorts. None of this lower stretch is on public land, however, and is virtually off limits to the average angler.

Traveling upstream to the point where the river is actually on the WMA puts the angler so far up the flow that the Hiwassee is a small headwaters stream. For the most part, here it is a shallow, swift, and rocky creek that offers very little holding water.

Unlike the lower areas of the river which are stocked heavily, no hatchery fish are released in the Swallow Creek WMA portion of the Hiwassee. This part of the river is also very heavily covered by foliage and not easily fished.

To get to the Hiwassee's headwaters go north on GA 75 from Helen to FS 283. Take a right and head east. This gravel road, which has a small sign for High Shoals at the intersection, runs sharply downhill off the highway and is easily missed when approached from the south. (If you reach Brasstown Creek and the historic marker for Brasstown Bald on GA 75, you have missed the turn.)

At .2 miles FS 233 fords the Hiwassee, and parking areas are located beside the creek and just past it.

HIGH SHOALS CREEK
SIZE: *Small to medium*
ACCESS: *Difficult*
SPECIES: *Wild brook trout*

High Shoals Creek is well known among sightseers in this part of Georgia, but not as a fishing hole. The waterfalls of the High Shoals Scenic Area attract crowds of hikers and campers to this flow, and few nature lovers leave the area disappointed.

Beautiful and relatively remote, High Shoals Scenic Area consists of several cataracts that thunder down the stream's course. The highest of these rises approximately 100 feet and, especially in the spring or at other times of heavy flows in the creek, is an awesome sight.

Among of the throngs of people that the falls attract, I have been the only angler on the stream on a Labor Day weekend. Though I was surrounded by hikers and campers I had the fish to myself. The fact that the creek is left off the trout brochure map is partially responsible for this, but the nature of the stream also contributes to its being neglected by anglers.

High Shoals rates as a medium-sized creek below the falls and only a small flow above them. In the upper part the rhododendron and other foliage forms the all-too-familiar canopy over the stream, and despite the presence of good holding water, fishing is very difficult. Below the falls the creek is more open, but it is cloaked in a perpetual spray from the cascades that make the rocks on the shore just as slippery as the ones in the stream.

As a result of these wet conditions, High Shoals is dangerous, and careless visitors have been killed. There are signs in the area placing the immediate vicinity of the falls off-limits; yet, over the years, some have chosen to ignore these warnings and venture the proverbial step closer for a better look. Several have plunged to their deaths.

Believe the signs! There is plenty of fishing water on this creek that does not necessitate getting close to any of the falls on the stream.

Another, more pleasant, feature of High Shoals Creek is that it is still home to native brook trout. Not a renovated stream, it has supported these wild little survivors continuously over the years. Of course, most of the fish in the creek are on the small side, but the portion of the stream below the falls has some pools that are big enough to promise the possibility of a larger fish or two. Brookies of up to 8 inches are a bit more common on High Shoals than on some of the other native trout streams.

To locate High Shoals Creek, continue on past the ford of the Hiwassee River on FS 283 for another mile. The parking area for the High Shoals Trail will appear on the left side of the road at a sharp right turn.

From this point the trail descends steeply downhill for 1 mile to the creek where there are a number of primitive camping sites along the stream. Although the path has switchbacks, it is still a strenuous climb coming out, especially when carrying a backpack.

CHAPTER EIGHTEEN

Lake Burton WMA

Trout fishing in the Peach State is not always an endeavor that is limited to those who can withstand the rigors of mountain hiking or tenuous perches on slippery rocks. Trout waters come in a number of shapes and forms in our state. On most of the wildlife management areas of the state, the Game and Fish Division of the Department of Natural Resources has made an effort to provide a variety of stream regulations and situations to allow for the broadest possible range of trout angling opportunities. Nowhere is this variety more apparent than on the Lake Burton WMA in northeast Georgia.

Spread across 12,600 acres of mountainous terrain in Rabun County on the northwest side of the lake from which it takes its name, the WMA contains three major trout streams. Dicks (not to be confused with the stream of the same name located on the Chestatee WMA), Moccasin, and Wildcat creeks make up the bulk of the fishery, although several feeder creeks also contain trout.

These streams—when combined with the lower stretch of Moccasin Creek in Moccasin Creek State Park, which adjoins but is not part of the WMA—run the gamut from true wilderness waters to creeks that are accessible to anglers in wheelchairs. The fish in the streams are quite varied as well.

Wild brown and rainbow trout are found on the area, as are native brook trout. Hatchery cousins of all three species are also stocked at various points.

For those folks who have more than one day to spend on the area's waters, there is also a variety of opportunities for food and lodging. As with most Georgia WMAs, primitive camping is allowed throughout the refuge. If your tastes run to "civilized" camping, Moccasin Creek State Park offers both tent and trailer sites. For those who desire even a bit more comfort, rustic cabin accommodations are available at LaPrades on Lake Burton just at the edge of the WMA. This regionally known resort, founded in 1925, provides bountiful, home-cooked, boardinghouse-style meals that are the ideal way to begin or end a day of trout fishing.

WILDCAT CREEK
    SIZE: *Small to medium*
    ACCESS: *Easy*
    SPECIES: *Stocked and wild brown and rainbow trout*

Wildcat is the southernmost of the streams on the Lake Burton WMA and is undoubtedly the best known. The reason for its popularity is easily recognized after only a cursory examination of the creek. It is classic Georgia mountain trout water. Easily accessible from FS 26 that parallels the stream for much of its length, the lower portion of the creek is composed of big, deep pools that seem built to order for the bait caster.

The fisheries managers from the Lake Burton Fish Hatchery add to the appeal of this stretch of water by generously stocking it with 8- to 14-inch rainbows on a weekly basis throughout the regular season. Do not expect to find solitude on Wildcat, for it is by far the most heavily fished stream on the WMA. After the weekly planting, the crowd can sometimes rival the turnout seen on opening day of the season.

Probably the most popular pool on the creek is the one at the foot of Sliding Rock. Although it is a most appealing bit

Lake Burton WMA

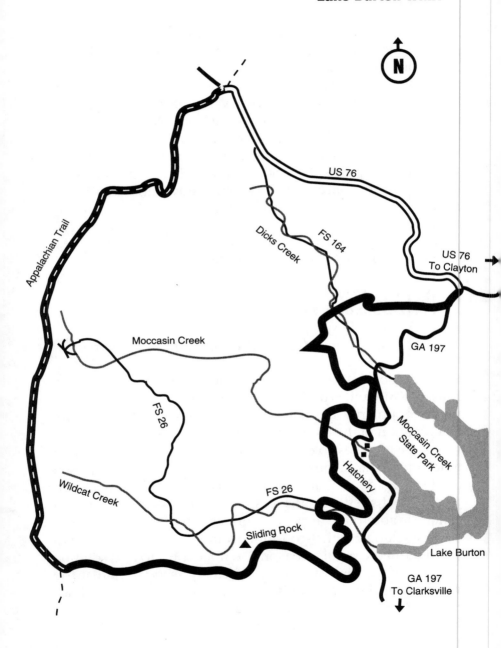

N

Appalachian Trail

US 76

Dicks Creek

FS 164

US 76
To Clayton

Moccasin Creek

GA 197

FS 26

Moccasin Creek
State Park

Hatchery

Wildcat Creek

FS 26

Sliding Rock

Lake Burton

GA 197
To Clarksville

of trout water that often holds plenty of fish, it also will usually be crowded with swimmers taking advantage of the natural slide created by the slippery rocks above the pool. On hot days the exciting 30-foot plunge into the icy water has enticed more than a few anglers as well.

If you are not tempted to join the swimmers or the throng of people casting on the other large pools on the creek, a third alternative is to probe the swift shoal areas between pools. The pockets in these whitewater areas hold fish that have strayed from the deeper waters where they were stocked. Being much less sought in this type of water, they will often be holdovers from earlier weeks.

Although there is plenty of room for fly casting on many of Wildcat's pools, the freshly stocked rainbows do not respond to flies as well as wild fish do. A more consistent approach to catching these fish is to present them with corn, salmon eggs, or earthworms. If artificials are used, an in-line spinner like the Rooster Tail or Panther Martin would be in order.

For the angler whose heart is set on landing a wild trout, some are present. Particularly for fly-fishers, the shoal areas of Wildcat will yield some stream-bred rainbows, though these will run only from 6 to 9 inches in length.

To find Wildcat Creek, travel north on GA 197 from Clarkesville. Immediately after passing LaPrades on the left, the road crosses Wildcat Creek at its flow into Lake Burton. Several hundred yards beyond the creek, turn left onto FS 26. About a mile up this road will be the edge of the WMA, which is clearly marked.

The road crosses the creek over four bridges before leaving the Wildcat Creek watershed and ending at a gate at the edge of the Tray Mountain Wilderness Area. This gate is 7 miles above the intersection of FS 26 and GA 197. There are two designated primitive campgrounds along the road, both of which are heavily used throughout the season.

Wildcat Creek is an excellent destination for the beginning angler or any who like their trout fishing on the less
strenuous side.

MOCCASIN CREEK

SIZE: *Small*
ACCESS: *Easy in state park, difficult on WMA*
SPECIES: *Stocked brook and rainbow trout,*
  wild brown and rainbow trout
SPECIAL REGULATIONS: *In state park stream open only*
  to anglers under 12 and to honorary license
  holders over 65 and to disabled persons

To speak of Moccasin Creek is actually to talk about two
distinct trout streams: the regulated waters of Moccasin Creek
State Park and the open waters farther upstream on the WMA.
Because of misconceptions concerning the special rules in
effect within the state park, even many knowledgeable trout
anglers are mystified when you start talking to them about
fishing this creek.

The last couple of hundred yards of Moccasin Creek as
it enters Lake Burton are not actually on the WMA, but they are
closely related to the WMA fishery. From GA 197 to Lake
Burton, Moccasin Creek is closed to all angling except by
children under 12 and by persons over 65 years of age who
hold an honorary fishing license. Additionally, the banks of
the stream here have been fitted with walking paths and a
platform to accommodate wheelchair anglers.

To insure good fishing, the creek receives substantial
weekly stockings of trout from the Lake Burton Hatchery that
adjoins the park. It is not uncommon for this stretch also to
receive surprise bonus stockings in the form of fish that are
simply allowed to exit the hatchery through its water-discharge
pipes into the creek.

The fish found in the regulated area of Moccasin Creek
usually run larger than in most other North Georgia stocked

waters. Rainbows of 12 to 15 inches do not even raise an eyebrow among the stream's regulars, and some heavyweight fish of up to 3 or 4 pounds also show up each summer.

If you qualify to fish these waters, they are an excellent choice in which to land a mess of frying trout. Almost any natural or artificial bait will usually produce some action.

For those of us who cannot use the regulated section, Moccasin Creek still offers a chance at a few trout. Across GA 197 and above a few hundred yards of private land is the southern edge of the WMA. From this point upstream Moccasin Creek is open to all anglers under the state's general trout regulations. At the junction of the highway and the dirt road leading to the WMA are signs explaining the restrictions for fishing Moccasin Creek and warning all others against fishing. This warning only applies, however, to the area downstream of the diversion dam that supplies the hatchery with water and does not affect the angling farther up the creek on the actual WMA lands.

The signs apparently have managed to create the impression among many that fishing is not permitted on Moccasin Creek except in the state park under the stringent regulations. As a result, the long stretch of water on the management area receives very light fishing pressure.

Above the hatchery Moccasin Creek does not receive any stockings of trout but contains a healthy, reproducing population of wild rainbows. Brown trout are also present, but in smaller numbers. Although the angling is tough, the rewards can be very satisfying.

When first encountered on the WMA, the creek appears too small and shallow to hold many fish of any size. As with other mountain streams, first impressions can be very misleading. A half mile upstream from the preserve's boundary the creek is much larger than it was at the edge, and a number of waterfalls and small drops create pools in which trout can hide.

The narrow valley the creek flows through makes the fishing rather difficult. There is a footpath along the bank that follows the bed of an old narrow-gauge railway, which once hauled out logs from timber camps deep in the mountains. Yet, the path is often many feet above the actual level of the stream and climbing down to fish can be an adventure in itself.

Because of the wariness of these wild fish and the usually very clear water, a good time to fish upper Moccasin Creek is after rains have clouded the water. Natural baits, such as crickets and worms, and small spinners and sinking flies can be extremely effective at those times. The trout in upper Moccasin Creek run on the small side, and anything more than 10 inches earns bragging rights on most days.

To locate Moccasin Creek continue north on GA 197 past Wildcat Creek for about 1 mile. Moccasin Creek flows under the road at the entrance to the state park, which is on the right. To the left and immediately *before* crossing the bridge over the creek is the dirt road leading to the WMA. There are several side roads branching off this track, but always keeping to the road straight ahead will put you on the stream at the public-access area. The road ends where it has been blocked at a large primitive camping clearing. The stream is to the right, with the road changing into the footpath and continuing straight ahead along the creek valley.

After leaving Wildcat Creek, FS 26 crosses the headwater of Moccasin Creek, but access from this point requires a long downhill hike to where Moccasin Creek is large enough for fishing.

DICKS CREEK

Size: *Small*
Access: *Difficult*
Species: *Wild brook, brown, and rainbow trout*

The final trout stream on the Lake Burton WMA is Dicks Creek. Unlike the popular stream on the Chestatee WMA that bears the same name, this creek is virtually unknown to most anglers. In fact, it does not even appear on the map of trout streams that is included in the Department of Natural Resources' "Guide To Georgia Trout Regulations" brochure.

Although it receives no stocked trout, the lower section of Dicks Creek, near the edge the WMA, has a fair population of wild rainbow trout and a sprinkling of browns. Farther upstream, the Game and Fish Division has renovated the headwaters as a wild brook-trout stream. There is some question as to how effective the renovation has been because, somehow, rainbow trout apparently have been reintroduced above the natural barrier falls that mark the downstream limit of the brook trout's range. The upper creek now has a mixed population that, to date, is still dominated by brookies.

These native Southern Appalachian brook trout are more a curiosity than anything else, since they rarely grow larger than 5 or 6 inches long. They are, however, plentiful in the upper creek and will readily attack baits, lures, or flies that are naturally presented.

Dicks Creek can be reached by traveling a mile north of Moccasin Creek State Park on GA 197. Immediately before crossing the highway bridge over the stream, a dirt road (FS 164) runs off to the left. It parallels the creek for about 1 mile to the edge of the WMA. Included in this distance are two fords that are passable for most cars at normal water levels. Once on the WMA, the road becomes very rough and fords the stream another 14 times in the next 3 miles before reaching the brookie water. At a sharp left turn just before ford No. 15, the barrier falls are visible upstream. Venturing beyond the edge of the WMA in a vehicle without 4-wheel drive is risky.

CHAPTER NINETEEN

Coleman River WMA

Just when you think that you have a stretch of water figured out and you know how to master the trout that swim there, it is time to get ready for a hefty slice of humble pie. A weekend trip to the Coleman River Wildlife Management Area a few summers back was an outing that very forcefully drove this point home for me. I was camping and fishing with Bob Townsend of Lithonia and a couple of other anglers on the headwaters of the Coleman River just south of the North Carolina border. We were also within the confines of the Georgia section of the Southern Nantahala Wilderness Area. We were exploring this particular stream because of the presence of native brook trout in its upper reaches.

As is standard in Georgia, any creek with native brookies is very small, bushy, and hard to fish. So it was with no small lapse of modesty that I pointed out to Bob, after the first day's fishing, that my fly-rod offerings had been attacked by more than a score of trout. On the other hand, his ultralight spinning tackle had fooled only a couple of fish.

The morning of the second day of our trip was reserved for trying the Tallulah River. This flow parallels the western boundary of the WMA and, in contrast to its tributary, the

Coleman River, is a fairly large stream that receives heavy stockings of catchable-sized rainbow trout. Having mastered the wild fish, I was certain that my cunning would wreak havoc on these naive stockers.

Three hours later, as I looked over Townsend's stringer of six rainbows in the 9- to 11-inch range, I enjoyed a heaping helping of the aforementioned humble pie. It was a fitting dessert to follow the crow that Bob dished out. Rather than catching trout, I had missed the single strike that my flies attracted. Meanwhile, the Rooster Tail spinner that Bob had fished proved deadly on the rainbows.

Of course, fate is a fickle fishing partner. During the afternoon we tried casting the portion of the Coleman just upstream from its junction with the Tallulah. It is open to fishing with artificial lures only and contains wild rainbow and brown trout.

Again the fishing took a 180-degree turn and I prospered, while Bob was getting skunked. Fortunately, we had both learned by this time that it is best simply to enjoy or endure the fate dealt to you and not to crow or moan about it.

The other lesson that we learned that weekend was not to give up hope when your favored fishing method is not producing on the Coleman River WMA. There is enough variety to the waters that a short drive or hike away will be a stream where the fish may be more receptive to your offerings.

The Coleman River WMA is composed of 11,000 acres of Chattahoochee National Forest lands in Rabun County. Located approximately 8 miles west of Clayton, the WMA is one of the more primitive natural areas left in the state. Considering the very rugged mountain terrain, including a section of the Southern Nantahala Wilderness Area, access to the trout streams is relatively easy. Good Forest Service gravel roads reach all the fishable waters on the WMA. These streams are all in the watershed of the Tallulah River and flow in a westerly or southwesterly direction (except the Tallulah itself, which flows from north to south).

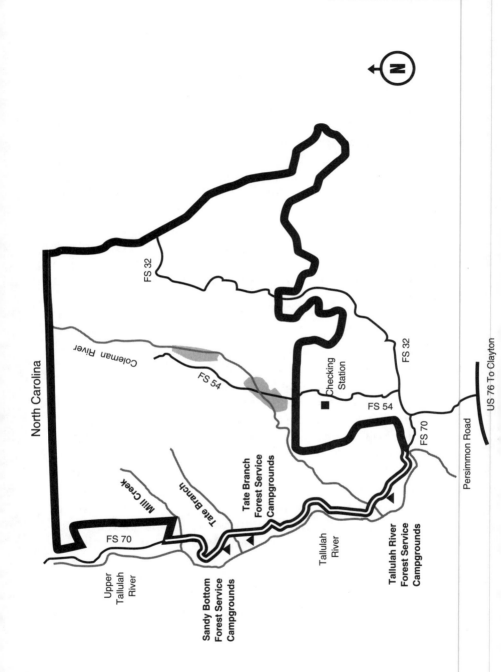

TALLULAH RIVER

SIZE: *Medium to large*

ACCESS: *Easy*

SPECIES: *Stocked brook trout, stocked and wild brown and rainbow trout*

SPECIAL REGULATIONS: *Open year-round*

The bulk of the western edge of the WMA is marked by FS 70. Because the Tallulah River flows just on the other side of the road and offers several miles of angling opportunities that are open to the public, it will be considered a part of the area's fishery.

The Tallulah River headwaters rise on the southern flanks of Standing Indian Mountain in North Carolina. From there it flows south into Georgia. In the section that parallels FS 70 along the edge of the WMA, the stream has some deep slow pools interspersed with tumbling shoal areas. It is ideal water for bait casting. All the traditional trout baits such as worms, corn, crickets, or cheese concoctions will work on the hatchery-raised rainbows that are released in the river throughout the season. Some brown and brook trout are occasionally stocked in this river as well.

The bulk of the fish caught will be in the 8- to 12-inch size. The pools, however, are big enough that a larger hold-over fish from earlier plantings is a possibility.

Light in-line spinners like the Rooster Tail, Mepps, or Panther Martin will also interest these trout. As my experience on the river proved, fly-fishing can be tough at times on the Tallulah. Nymphs or wet flies are probably the better bets in the larger pools. Fish them deep and slow, just off the bottom.

When approaching the Tallulah on FS 70, be aware that the stream is on private property when you first see it. You cannot fish this part of the river without the landowners' permission. Farther up FS 70 there is the Tallulah River Forest Service campground near the mouth of the Coleman River, and fishing in this area is open to the public. There are also two other Forest Service campgrounds farther upstream, at the junction of the Tallulah with Tate Branch and at Sandy Bottom.

To get to the Tallulah River travel 8 miles west on US 76 from Clayton to the intersection with Persimmon Road. This paved road enters the highway from the right. The Tallulah Persimmon Fire Department building will be on the right as you turn onto the road. At this point Persimmon is also designated as the beginning of FS 70.

Stay on Persimmon Road for 4.2 miles to the intersection with FS 32. FS 70 goes to the left and FS 32 to the right. A sign at this junction directs travelers to the left for the Tallulah River. The next .8 miles of the road is paved to the Forest Service's first campground by the river.

COLEMAN RIVER

SIZE: *Small*

ACCESS: *Moderate to difficult*

SPECIES: *Wild brook, brown, and rainbow trout*

SPECIAL REGULATIONS: *Artificial lures only from stream's mouth up to FS 54 bridge*

Although called a river, the Coleman is only a small stream. Or, more correctly for the trout angler, it is two streams in one. From its mouth on the Tallulah upstream to the FS 54 bridge it is open only to artificial-lure fishing. Access to this stretch is good, but moderately strenuous, via the Coleman River Scenic Trail that parallels the creek.

The water in the river is generally clear, and the fish can be quite spooky. Especially on bright, sunny days it is best to probe the pockets of water in shaded recesses against the boulders to provoke a strike.

The wild rainbows (no stocking is presently being done on this stream) will run from 7 to 10 inches long. Although brown trout are present, they are hard to catch. Their natural reluctance to fall victim to usual fishing tactics and the crystal waters make them tough customers.

Regardless of the species sought, fishing the calmer pools on the Coleman will prove very frustrating because the trout will see the angler long before the angler can put a hook in front of them. Often the better tactic is to fish the broken pocket water. Look for those spots where the current sweeps around a boulder or between two rocks. If the water is 18 inches or deeper, the odds are good that a fish will be holding in the lie watching for an easy meal to float by. The broken surface of the water in the moving current will shield the angler's approach.

The upper portion of the Coleman—above FS 54 and a small patch of private land—is an altogether different stream. An artificial barrier and waterfall protect a population of wild brook trout from encroachment by other species. These native fish rarely get as large as 8 inches and will usually be from 5 to 6 inches. They will hit virtually anything cast into the pool that does not frighten them. Still, the fishing is not easy because of the small size of the pools and runs and the extremely congested streamside foliage.

In essence, fishing the upper Coleman can be an interesting challenge, but it is a waste of time for the angler planning to have a trout dinner at the end of the day.

To reach the mouth of the Coleman River follow the same directions as for the Tallulah. The Coleman empties into that larger stream at the Tallulah River campground.

TATE BRANCH
SIZE: *Small*
ACCESS: *Easy to Moderate*
SPECIES: *Wild brook trout*

Tate Branch is a small stream that empties into the Tallulah River farther north than the Coleman. The last hundred yards or so of the branch flows through the Tate Branch Forest Service campground and under FS 70 before joining the Tallulah.

Just upstream of the road and camping area a barrier falls constructed to limit upstream movement of fish marks the beginning of a section renovated for wild brook trout. There is a good footpath along the south side of the creek.

Tate Branch is bushy and very tight to fish above the campground, but it is also the most easily reached of the native trout creeks in the state. For that reason, it appears to get relatively heavy angling pressure for a brookie stream, although the pressure it receives would rate only as light on a stocked stream. The trout in the stream run small even by brook-trout standards, with most of the fish being 4 or 5 inches long.

To find Tate Branch, follow the directions for the mouth of the Coleman River, then proceed another 4 miles north on FS 70. The road crosses the creek at the Tate Branch campground.

MILL CREEK
SIZE: *Small*
ACCESS: *Moderate*
SPECIES: *Wild brook trout*

The final stream on the Coleman River WMA is Mill Creek, which is very seldom visited by anglers and at FS 70 is quite small. At the bridge, there are several signs just upstream of the road identifying the edge of the WMA and the boundary of the national forest lands. Above this point it is necessary practically to crawl up a tunnel of vegetation through which the creek flows. This first impression is undoubtedly enough to discourage most anglers from proceeding. The trick on this creek is to park at the bridge, then walk a few yards farther north on the road. Watch for a trail entering from the right at the point where an old logging road once entered the main road. Although the logging road's entrance was bulldozed long ago and is now overgrown and steep, it is easily recognized. This path follows the stream and bypasses the unfishable lower part of the creek, giving access to water that is a little bit more open and has some interesting pools.

Mill Creek is another of the Coleman River area's native brook-trout streams and is actually the best of the lot. It has plenty of fish, with some reaching the 7- to 8-inch range. Still, the fishing is in close quarters and difficult and will not produce a limit catch for the frying pan. This is a stream to fish for the adventure, not to fill the larder.

Approaching Mill Creek on FS 70 requires driving an additional half mile north of Tate Branch to the final Forest Service campground on the road. This recreation area is located at Sandy Bottom. Just beyond the campsites there is a patch of private land that extends along both sides of the road. There is also a sign announcing the city limits of Tate City. (Population 32, according to the sign on my last visit) The village consists of a handful of farms and residences spread along the next half mile of road.

At Mill Creek—there is no sign at the bridge, but it is the first creek beyond Tate City—Forest Service land once again includes the right shoulder of the road, and there is room to park a car or two just before crossing the bridge.

CHAPTER TWENTY

Lake Russell WMA

Lake Russell WMA is almost a backyard fishery. Three neighboring municipalities—Baldwin, Cornelia, and Mt. Airy —lie on the western edge of the WMA, with the last actually bordering the preserve. Just to the northeast, is the town of Toccoa.

The WMA is situated on 17,000 acres of land in Habersham, Stephens, and Banks counties in the northeast quadrant of the state. The property, owned by private timber companies or the Forest Service, lies within the confines of the Chattahoochee National Forest.

Although technically part of Georgia's mountain geophysical region, the area is better characterized as foothill country. Access is good to the southern edge of the WMA via paved roads. In the northern portion, well-maintained Forest Service gravel roads make travel easy.

The easy access and variety of camping, fishing, and other recreational opportunities make this WMA a prime summer destination, particularly for family camping groups. The area can become rather crowded on spring or summer weekends.

As a fishing destination, Lake Russell WMA has its drawbacks. There are only limited trout-angling opportunities available, and these are of the put-and-take variety. By the way, Lake Russell, for which this management area is named, does not actually lie on the WMA, but is a warm-water fishery to the southwest on Nancytown Creek. Also, this Lake Russell should not be confused with the much larger reservoir located in the same part of the state on the Savannah River.

NANCYTOWN LAKE
SIZE: *Large*
ACCESS: *Easy*
SPECIES: *Stocked rainbow trout*

Approaching the Lake Russell WMA from the east through Cornelia, the first trout water encountered is Nancytown Lake. Just upstream of Lake Russell on Nancytown Creek, the cooler waters of Nancytown Lake are supplied with catchable-sized rainbows throughout the fishing season. These stockers are most often caught by anglers on the bank casting a wide variety of natural baits. Undoubtedly, the trout will also attack spinners and other artificial lures as well.

To get to Nancytown Lake, head out of Mt. Airy traveling north on US 123. Watch for Red Root Road (FS 61) on the right and the sign at the intersection for Lake Russell Recreation Area. Turn right and follow the signs along the paved road to get to Nancytown Lake.

MIDDLE FORK OF BROAD RIVER
SIZE: *Small*
ACCESS: *Easy to moderate*
SPECIES: *Stocked brown and rainbow trout*

The Middle Fork of the Broad River is the only trout stream on the Lake Russell WMA, and it is marginal at best. Instead of the tumbling mountain brooks that trout anglers are used to seeing, the Middle Fork is more of a small, meandering valley stream. While the flow of the river is rather slow, it does

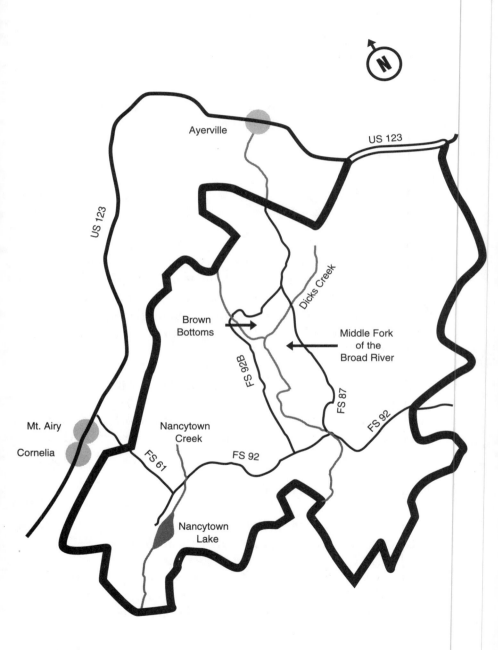

Lake Russell WMA

164

offer some deeper water in bends and some enticing-looking undercut banks.

There is no natural reproduction of trout in the river, but it is heavily stocked during the summer. It is also heavily fished by campers in the area, and there appears to be very little, if any, carryover of fish from year to year. Most of the fish are caught on bait, but spinning lures do take a fair share of the rainbows landed on the Middle Fork. Although two gravel Forest Service roads parallel the river on either side through most of the WMA, they are not right on the stream bank. Some walking along streamside trails is required to cover much of the water.

One area of heavy usage of the river is at Browns Bottom on FS 92B in the northern half of the WMA. Where the road crosses the river, there are several primitive campsites and easy access to the water. As far as primitive camping is concerned, all the roads in the vicinity of the river have campsites scattered along them.

Access to the lower end of the Middle Fork on the WMA is reached by continuing past the turnoff for Nancytown Lake on Red Root Road, which changes to gravel and is designated as FS 92 beyond the intersection. Just before it is joined by FS 87 (Sellers Road), FS 92 crosses the river and then turns south to parallel it for a short distance.

To get to the northern, upper end of the Middle Fork, turn left onto FS 92B from FS 92 about halfway between Nancytown Lake and the FS 92 bridge over the Middle Fork. This spur leads to the west side of the river and Browns Bottom. (Eventually FS 92B intersects FS 87 and runs into Ayersville at US 123.)

Dicks Creek, which is a fair-sized feeder stream that flows into the Middle Fork at Brown's Bottom, looks more like a trout stream than the main flow. It is not normally stocked, however, and is considered to be too small and gets too warm in the summer to be planted with fish. Dicks Creek was experimentally stocked with fingerling brown trout at one time, but the effort did not prove successful.

CHAPTER TWENTY-ONE

Warwoman WMA

In the extreme northeast corner of the Peach State in Rabun County lies the Warwoman WMA. It is composed of 15,800 acres of extremely rugged and mountainous terrain on US Forest Service land. Until recently, the area's trout streams fell into two categories: those that were difficult to find and the one that was difficult to reach. Fortunately, Rabun County now has put up some road signs at intersections important to trout anglers, somewhat easing the first problem.

Three of the four creeks that make up this fishery have decent access, but you have to know where you are going in order to find them. They are not streams that you are likely to stumble onto by accident. All four flow southeasterly to empty into Warwoman Creek below the WMA lands, and that creek, in turn, flows into the Chattooga River. We'll begin our discussion of the WMA waters on the western end of the preserve and work to the east.

TUCKALUGE CREEK
Size: *Small*
Access: *Easy to moderate*
Species: *Wild brook trout*

Tuckaluge Creek is another of the streams that the state has renovated to support wild brook trout. Unlike some of the other creeks in this category, Tuckaluge offers some good pools in which the fish can hide. It is also a brook-trout creek easily reached by car.

As usual, the vast majority of fish will be small, but brookies of up to 8 inches are present. The fishing in the lower part of the creek near the Warwoman Road edge of the WMA is not particularly difficult for anyone who is familiar with small-stream angling. In places there is even room to make some short back casts with a fly rod.

Although the stream receives some fishing pressure, the small size of the fish apparently keeps this to a minimum. Some primitive camping sites are visible at the edge of the WMA and appear to be frequently used.

To locate Tuckaluge Creek, travel 6.2 miles east on Warwoman Road from its intersection with US 23/441 in Clayton. At this point Tuckaluge Road joins Warwoman Road from the left. This gravel road runs through some open pastures, and the creek (there is no sign identifying it) is visible a few yards ahead.

Turn onto this gravel track, which is designated FS 153 on maps but only has a sign identifying it as Tuckaluge Road. Proceed 3/4 of a mile north to the edge of the WMA. This boundary is marked with a large wooden sign just before you cross the bridge over Tuckaluge. There is room to park on either side of the bridge. The Forest Service road continues to follow the creek up into the WMA.

WALNUT FORK CREEK

SIZE: *Small*
ACCESS: *Moderate to difficult*
SPECIES: *Wild brown and rainbow trout*
SPECIAL REGULATIONS: *Artificial lures only*

Warwoman WMA

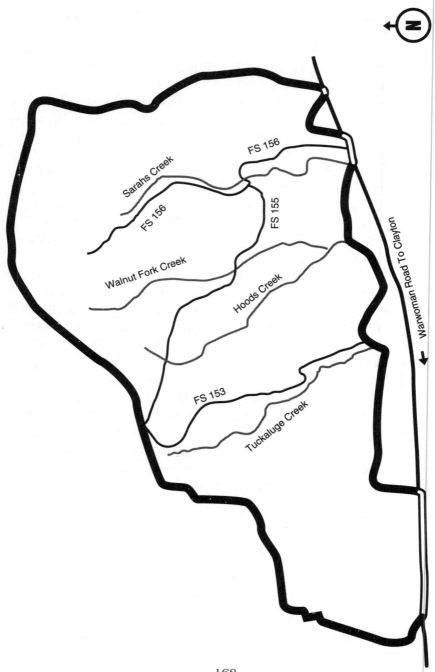

The next stream to the west is Walnut Fork Creek. This small stream is open for artificial-lure-only angling down to the edge of the Warwoman WMA. Above that boundary, all of Walnut Fork is on public land.

Although fairly difficult to find, Walnut Fork can be reached by car at points. There are plenty of stream-bred rainbow trout in the flow, with most being in the 6- to 8- inch range. Brown trout are also present and a bit more prevalent than in most mountain streams. These fish turn up regularly in sizes of more than 9 inches.

To get to Walnut Fork, travel 1.3 miles past Tuckaluge Creek on Warwoman Road and cross Walnut Fork Creek (there is no sign identifying the creek at the crossing). This portion of the water, however, is below the WMA and on private property.

The maps of the WMA provided by the Game and Fish Division show a dirt track running up the western side of this stream. The entrance to this track is by Henry Page Road, which runs north off of Warwoman Road just before you reach the creek. One-half mile later, where it passes the last houses, the road becomes very rough and is passable only in dry weather. Just past this point the road enters the WMA, and the stream is 1/4 mile from the beginning of the rough portion of the road. The road fords the stream and becomes a hiking trail at this point.

Another option for getting to Walnut Fork Creek is to travel 1.7 miles past the creek on Warwoman Road and take a left on FS 156. This road is very steep at the junction and is paved for the first 0.1 mile up the mountain. A small sign at the junction has the road number on it, as well as a road sign identifying it at Sarah's Creek Road.

The road turns to gravel at the top of the mountain and continues north for 2.1 miles to an intersection with FS 155, which also has a small sign identifying it. This intersection is just beyond a ford on Sarahs Creek. Turn left and go 1.3 miles over the ridge to Walnut Fork Creek. At this point you cannot see the creek, but a sign by the road identifies it and warns about the artificial-lure restriction. You can hear the creek going over a small waterfall in the woods to the left of the road.

The road parallels the creek for .6 miles to a bridge, then continues up on the ridge between the Walnut Fork and Hoods creek valleys. The area where the road runs along Walnut Fork Creek offers several primitive camping sites.

HOODS CREEK

SIZE: *Small*
ACCESS: *Difficult*
SPECIES: *Wild brown and rainbow trout*
SPECIAL REGULATIONS: *Artificial lures only*

Hoods Creek is the exception on Warwoman WMA in that not only is it hard to find, but also it is almost inaccessible. Hoods is a small creek that flows into Walnut Fork Creek a few hundred yards above the southern edge of the WMA. It is heavily canopied but does have some long, calm pools, as well as some in-stream structures. Hoods Creek is restricted to the use of artificial lures only on the WMA, which combines with the difficult access to limit fishing pressure.

The creek gets no hatchery-stocked fish and supports wild, stream-bred populations of both brown and rainbow trout. Anglers who put out the effort to reach Hoods Creek should be rewarded with some interesting wild trout fishing.

To find Hoods Creek, follow the directions for the lower portion of Walnut Fork Creek, then walk a few hundred yards north on the hiking trail along the Walnut Fork. Signs are posted on both creeks at their junction, identifying each and noting the artificial-lure regulations.

SARAHS CREEK

SIZE: *Small to medium*
ACCESS: *Easy*
SPECIES: *Stocked and wild brown and rainbow trout*

Sarahs Creek is the only stream on the Warwoman that is regularly stocked with catchable-sized trout. Access is not particularly difficult from the standpoints of terrain and quality of the roads, which helps explain why the stream is under intense pressure from heavy usage by both anglers and campers.

On the WMA portion of the flow, Sarahs Creek is a medium-sized trout stream. It has pools that are 20 to 30 feet wide and 3 to 4 feet deep in many spots. Another characteristic of the stream is that it is surprisingly level to be in such a rugged and mountainous area. The valley through which it flows is so gently sloped that several large stream structures were installed in the creek some years ago in order to give it some distinct pools. In many spots through the camping areas, Sarahs Creek is so open that fly casts of up to 50 or 60 feet are possible.

The creek's size and the regular stockings of rainbow trout have combined to attract large numbers of visitors to this stream. In fact, the Forest Service points to this creek as one of several in the Chattahoochee National Forest threatened by heavy usage. The riparian environment is being seriously degraded by the continued presence of large numbers of campers in a relatively small space.

The average trout found in the pools on Sarahs Creek are stocked rainbows from 8 to 10 inches in length. They can be caught by virtually any method—bait, spinner, or fly—but like most hatchery-reared fish, they are usually quite reluctant to come to the surface for a dry fly. Wet flies or nymphs will be more productive on this creek.

There are some wild fish in Sarahs Creek. Undoubtedly, the heavy angling pressure keeps the larger wild fish thinned out, but many pools hold a few stream-reared rainbow trout of 6 to 7 inches, and some small browns also turn up.

All in all, most days of fishing on Sarahs Creek will lack the mystique of a wilderness adventure, and probably there will be more people around than usual for pursuing trout. Still, it is a good place to go looking for a limit of stockers for a fish dinner.

To reach Sarahs Creek, follow the same directions as those used for the upper portion of Walnut Fork Creek. The signs on Warwoman Road on either side of the junction with FS 156 are marked Sarah Creek. The road sign at the intersection identifies FS 156 as Sarah's Creek Road. Finally, maps of the WMA identify the stream as Sarahs Creek. In spite of these variations of spelling, all sources refer to the same creek, which the Forest Service and the Georgia Game and Fish Division identify as Sarahs Creek.

Just before the intersection of FS 156 with FS 155 you go through the heart of the most-used camping areas. Near the road junction, FS 156 has a paved ford across the creek. It is suitable for passage by any type of vehicle.

Sarahs Creek is along the left side of the road when first encountered, but it parallels the road for a long way above the ford and intersection mentioned earlier. After crossing the ford, stay on FS 156 with the creek on the right.

CHAPTER TWENTY-TWO

Loose Ends

There are a few additional ponds and streams that merit at least a mention in this guide. Some are located in Georgia state parks or are on Chattahoochee National Forest land.

PINELOG WMA

Flowing through the heart of the 14,913-acre Pinelog WMA, Stamps Creek is large enough to handle a few anglers, is stocked with catchable rainbow trout, and is open to public fishing. It should also be noted, however, that the creek is a very marginal lowland stream that is better habitat for warm-water species and, during the summer, may not have any trout in it. For those reasons, even though it is a wildlife management area, it is not included with the others.

To reach Pinelog WMA and Stamps Creek, take US 411 north from US 41 for 7 miles to the village of White. Turn right on Stamps Creek Road, and at 3.7 miles the checking station is on the left. Stamps Creek flows beside the station and is open to fishing upstream of the road.

AMICALOLA FALLS STATE PARK

This state park lying on the Gilmer-Dawson county line contains a portion of Little Amicalola Creek, including the highest waterfall in Georgia. The portion of the creek from the foot of the falls down to the edge of the park is stocked during the regular trout season. The stream is very small, and some in-stream structure work has been done along it to improve the trout habitat and create holding water. These spots offer the best fishing holes.

Little Amicalola Creek does not rate as a primary trout-fishing destination, but offers a diversion to the angler who is visiting there. The park is located on GA 52 between Ellijay and Dahlonega at the crossroads of Juno.

LAKE WINFIELD SCOTT

Lake Winfield Scott is a National Forest Recreation Area located on GA 180 in Union County between Blairsville and Dahlonega. The lake lies adjacent to Coopers Creek WMA.

Built during the 1930s by the Civilian Conservation Corps, this old lake is stocked during the trout season with keeper-sized trout and is open to fishing under standard trout regulations. Winfield Scott is best suited to bait or spin fishing.

VOGEL STATE PARK

This state park is located near the intersection of US 19 and GA 180 in Union County. The trout fishery in the park consists of put-and-take stocking of Lake Trahlyta. The lake is surrounded by picnic and day-use areas, as well as camp-grounds. There is also a swimming beach and rental paddle boats on the lake. With such multiple use of the waters, the fishing is not the major attraction.

Pan-sized rainbow trout are released into the lake throughout the season, and an occasional holdover fish of 18 to 20 inches will turn up on a lucky angler's stringer.

UNICOI STATE PARK

Lying just to the north of Helen in White County, Unicoi is one of the largest state parks in north Georgia. Although Unicoi Lake is similar to Lake Winfield Scott and Lake Trahlyta as far as size and condition of its waters are concerned, it does not receive stockings of trout. Smith Creek that feeds the lake is stocked on a regular basis along its flow upstream of the lake as far as the culvert near the rental cabins.

Above the cabins, stocking is no longer done and a good population of small wild trout exists. Since the planting of trout has ceased in this portion of the creek, fishing pressure appears to have declined sharply.

Some stocking takes place below Unicoi Lake, where Smith Creek is basically a lowland stream, flowing down a relatively level valley. Especially during the summer the creek can become lukewarm by the time it runs out of the park to empty into the Chattahoochee River near Robertstown.

To find Unicoi State Park, go north of Helen on GA 75 to the intersection with GA 356 and turn right. This highway runs though the park and across the dam at Unicoi Lake.

SOQUE RIVER

This major tributary of the Chattahoochee River is a trout fishery where it flows through Habersham County north of Clarkesville. It is big water by Georgia standards and is quite tempting to any angler crisscrossing the stream on GA 197. Unfortunately, the Soque (spelled Soquee on Forest Service maps of the Chattahoochee National Forest) is located almost exclusively on private property. Because the bulk of these holdings are posted, very little of the Soque is open to the public.

The only section of the river on public land is a portion running through Forest Service holdings between Crow and Yellow mountains. For a short section—in the vicinity of the junction of GA 197 and FS 268—public land straddles the river and then continues downstream a bit farther on the west bank.

The Soque is stocked with catchable-sized trout several times during the fishing season, mainly on the public-access area. The portion of the river on public land is open during the regular trout season.

WARWOMAN CREEK

Rising in the Warwoman Dell area near the town of Clayton, Warwoman Creek flows for a number of miles as a small stream through a valley dominated by private farmlands. None of this upper area, which is paralleled by Warwoman Road and lies to the southeast of the Warwoman WMA, is open to the public. Eventually the stream bends away from the paved road and enters US Forest Service land for its last mile down to the Chattooga River at Earls Ford.

Through this public land the creek is of medium size and flows sluggishly through deep pools, broken by short rapids. The quality of the trout habitat is only marginal, but the stream is heavily stocked with hatchery-reared fish. It is also heavily fished, as evidenced by the worn condition of the banks and the number of campsites along it.

On occasion, Warwoman Creek produces a surprise like the 8-pound, 23-inch rainbow pulled from its waters in April of 1992. The trout was not a released brood-stock fish, but a holdover from earlier stocking.

Access to Warwoman Creek is via Earls Ford Road, a dirt track that runs off the southeast side of Warwoman Road between Walnut Fork Creek and FS 156. At 3/4 mile Earls Ford Road crosses Warwoman Creek to enter the Forest Service land and parallels the creek for 0.5 mile.

PANTHER CREEK

The final piece of trout water in North Georgia to be covered is Panther Creek in Habersham and Stephens counties. The public-access part of the stream flows on Forest Service land between US 23/441 and FS 182.

Panther Creek, a tributary of the Tugaloo River, is a very scenic creek but is marginal trout water. There are several waterfalls along the flow. These attract a lot of hikers to the trail that follows the entire length of the stream's course on public land.

Rainbow trout are stocked in the stream several times each spring and summer. The creek is open to fishing 12 months of the year.

To locate Panther Creek go north on US 23/441 from Clarkesville through the little community of Turnerville. Just beyond this village you come to the creek, which is marked with a sign for the Panther Creek Recreation Area. The trail and public land are on the right side of the road.

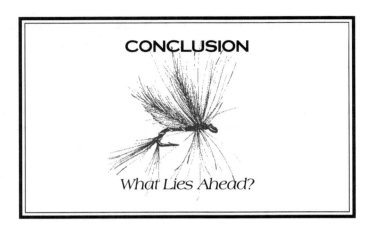

CONCLUSION

What Lies Ahead?

In trying to predict the future, it is possible to see either good times or great disasters looming on the horizon. There are so many variables to be considered that the future of trout fishing in Georgia depends largely on the choices we as a society make in both the short and long terms.

On the one hand, things look very bright and promising for the trout streams of Georgia. Much of the highlands of the northern third of the state are protected by the Chattahoochee National Forest. Under current policies, the developer's bull-dozer presents no threat to these lands.

Even more encouraging, during the last two decades we have added thousands of acres of land to the federal wilder-ness system in the Peach State. There seems to be a refreshing new awareness on the part of all Georgians that wild, pristine environments are worth saving.

Another plus for Georgia's cold-water fisheries are the activities of groups such as Trout Unlimited. Volunteers put in countless hours working in conjunction with state and federal authorities to improve and protect the trout habitat of our streams.

Today's fisheries managers show a dedication to the idea that "more" is not always the same as "better." Thus, the hatchery trucks no longer stop at every stream. Some areas are managed as wild trout streams, while others are set aside as put-and-take fisheries.

Some people would argue that we should strive for nothing but wild, stream-bred fisheries, but I believe that such a policy would be very difficult to implement and most likely self-defeating. It is estimated that there are more than 200,000 trout anglers who fish in Peach State waters each year. Natural reproduction could support this level of participation only through a strict catch-and-release regulation on all waters, and I doubt that such a program is feasible. If it were implemented, how many anglers would we lose from the sport? How long can any resource continue to prosper and enjoy protection if it loses its constituency?

At present the state is stocking more than a million trout in our streams annually, which works out to only five keepers per angler each year. If this is the investment needed to keep the public eye on our resource and sport, to maintain a large enough following to guarantee protection of the streams and fish, it seems a small price to pay.

Having made these points for a bright future, let me take a moment to consider the alternatives. The disadvantage of having a large constituency is that the resource gets a lot of pressure. Some of the most alluring trout-fishing destinations, such as Jacks River Falls, Sarahs Creek, and the Chattahoochee River, are coming under increasingly abusive pressure simply because there are so many people wanting to camp, hike, or fish near these natural treasures.

No one likes the idea of having to limit access to any of our resources or to impose user fees so that funds can be raised to rehabilitate areas suffering from heavy visitation. Still one or both of these strategies seem to be in the future. Up until now the sale of hunting stamps has provided the vast majority of funds for upkeep on the areas that contain most of our public trout waters. Sooner or later the angler, camper and hiker will be asked to share these costs.

There are danger signals in the very condition of our environment in the southern United States as well. For almost 20 years now there have been warnings about acid rain and its potentially destructive effects on our trout fisheries. Probably the most disturbing aspect of this threat is that we still do not know for sure exactly what the problem is or how to address it.

While environmental groups clamor for an end to the release of industrial pollution into the air, no one—not business, government, or environmentalists—seems eager to foot the bill for the new technologies to correct the problems or to pay to clean up damage already done. We have yet even to reach agreement as to the dimensions of the problems. Less finger pointing and more research on the subject would be refreshing.

Mike Gennings, the director of fisheries for Georgia, discussed "global warming" in a recent interview. He noted that some researchers studying the phenomenon predict that within perhaps two decades the South will be so hot that trout water will descend no farther into the region than the mountains of Virginia. Again there is argument over what part humankind plays in the problem, as well as just how big the problem is, or whether a problem exists at all.

Facing this triumvirate of thorny issues—overuse, economics, and the environment—it is easy to take a very bleak view of the future of Georgia's trout fishery.

What can we as anglers do? Above all, stay informed and get involved. Do not simply hide from the problems by spending a great day on the creek bank, going home, and taking trout fishing for granted. Neglect is a surefire prescription for the problems to get worse. Anglers must let elected officials hear from them on issues that affect—positively or negatively—our wild places and our sport.

We can speak up as individuals and through such groups as Trout Unlimited and the Georgia Conservancy. These organizations have track records of practical involvement and solid achievement in protecting the areas where wild trout live. If we all do our part, we can insure that future generations will have the same variety and quality of trout angling that we enjoy today in the Peach State.

Appendix

GENERAL TROUT REGULATIONS

In order to fish for trout, all anglers 16 years of age or older are required to have a current Georgia fishing license and a trout stamp in their possession. Children under 16 do not need a license. Residents of Georgia who are 65 years of age or older and anyone who is totally blind, or permanently and totally disabled may obtain an honorary license by applying to the Georgia Game and Fish Division. Honorary license holders do not have to possess a trout stamp. Anglers in Georgia state parks must have a fishing license but do not need a trout stamp.

The general trout season in Georgia runs from the last weekend in March to the end of October each year. This season applies to all waters that the Game and Fish Division has designated as trout waters, unless the stream appears on the list of year-round trout waters.

Trout anglers are restricted to using one hand-held rod and reel and cannot use live bait-fish in any Georgia trout stream. The creel limit is 8 trout per day, regardless of species.

The Department of Natural Resources publishes the Georgia Guide to Trout Regulations each year, containing lists of the designated trout waters and the year-round streams. Copies are available from most fishing tackle and sporting goods outlets in North Georgia each March, or the brochure can be requested from the nearest Fisheries Office of the Game and Fish Division.

SAFETY FIRST

The first dangers that most people mention in connection with the North Georgia area that contains trout streams are bears and poisonous snakes. The mountains do contain bears, but these creatures are very shy and rarely encountered. In more than 20 years of visiting the most remote areas of North Georgia, I have never seen a bear. Anglers who have reported encounters generally get only a fleeting glimpse of the animal in full retreat.

While copperheads and timber rattlesnakes are seen occasionally, they, too, will readily flee rather than face a human being. They represent a danger only when startled at close range or inadvertently cornered. Being alert to one's surroundings is the most effective method of avoiding these snakes.

The major danger to trout anglers on Northern Georgia streams is posed by the slippery rocks, which, at times, must be waded upon. While bear attacks are unheard of in Georgia and snakebites rare, serious injuries to anglers who fall on slick rocks occur all too frequently. Wearing felt-soled wading boots while fishing is the best precaution against such injuries.

Other dangers few people think about while fishing, until they find themselves in trouble, are the hornet and yellow jacket nests that are plentiful in the spring and summer. An encounter with a swarm of angry hornets whose nest you have just hooked can ruin a fishing trip in the same way that stepping on a yellow jacket nest will.

Hornets often build their nests in trees overhanging mountain streams, while yellow jackets burrow into the banks along the creek. Again, being aware of one's surroundings at all times is the best preventive measure.

BE PREPARED

In the event an accident occurs while trout fishing, the consequences are much less severe if you are prepared to deal with the situation. Above all, using common sense will prevent most accidents before they can happen. When possible, take someone fishing with you. There is safety in numbers, particularly in remote regions. If you do go alone, make sure someone knows exactly where you are going and how long you will be there.

Two pieces of equipment that should be part of every angler's gear are a first aid kit and a whistle. The kit can take care of many minor injuries, while a whistle can be a lifesaver in alerting others to your distress in case of a major mishap.

One caution concerning first aid is also necessary. While it may be prudent to carry a snakebite kit when venturing into remote wilderness areas, it should be used as a last resort. Cutting a vein or artery, or misusing a tourniquet can be more dangerous than a snakebite. If you are within an hour's travel time of a hospital when bitten, forget the snakebite kit and seek medical attention at once.

About the Author

Jimmy Jacobs, a lifelong resident of Georgia, has spent the last twenty years fishing for trout in the streams of north Georgia. He holds a degree in journalism from Georgia State University and is editor of *Georgia Sportsman, Alabama Game and Fish*, and *Florida Game and Fish* magazines. He has written on the subject of trout fishing in Georgia for *Fly Fisherman* as well as numerous other outdoor publications, and won Georgia Outdoor Writers Association Excellence in Craft Awards in 1990, 1991, and 1992.